student athletes
and ear

UNDERSTA... ...RECRUITING PROCESS!

"Student athletes must understand that the recruiting process starts with academics, and it begins in their freshman year. If students don't meet NCAA academic and eligibility requirements, they will not receive sports scholarships regardless of how great their athletic ability."

**Mike Stoops,
associate head football coach,
University of Oklahoma, the 2000 national champions**

"This book tells it like it is. The recruiting process that leads to athletic scholarships and financial aid is all about numbers—your GPA, your height, your weight, your speed, how many scholarships each sport has to offer, etc."

**Mark Stoops,
defensive backs coach,
University of Miami, FL, the 2001 national champions**

"Young athletes need to know that athletic scholarships are not given to just good players on great high-school teams. There is so much more involved concerning the recruiting process. They need to know that being an attractive recruit requires a 12-month-a-year commitment to becoming a better student athlete."

**Matt Wilhelm,
All-American linebacker,
The Ohio State University, the 2002 national champions**

Paul Maguire, ESPN NFL analyst (L), with author Mark Bercik.

"Today's young athletes should be making sure they acquire a college education first and foremost!

"Their 'Plan B' should be playing sports at the next level—it should NOT be their 'Plan A.'"

**Paul Maguire,
ESPN Sunday Night NFL analyst**

America's Complete Sports Scholarship Guide

(Athletic and Academic)

Subtitle: Giving Something Back to the Game

by **Mark Bercik**

A "how-to" guide to help you clearly understand the athletic recruiting process and how it leads to

sports scholarships and financial aid!

For parents and student athletes (ages 8-18) of all sports.

Published by: America Sports Publishing
Brookfield, Ohio

Title: ***America's Complete SPORTS SCHOLARSHIP GUIDE***

Subtitle: *Giving Something Back to the Game*

Copyright © 2003 by Mark Bercik

Edited by Diane Wilding

All rights reserved. No part of this book may be reproduced, republished, distributed, or transmitted in any form or by any means, electronic or mechanical, including photocopies, recordings, or any information storage or retrieval system without prior permission in writing from the author. Requests for permission to make copies of any part of this work may be mailed to Mark Bercik, Sports Scholarship Guide, P. O. Box 132, Brookfield OH 44403, or e-mailed to Mark@AthleticScholarshipBook.com.

Published by America Sports Publishing

Printed in the United States of America

Publisher's Cataloging-in-Publication
(Provided by ***Quality Books, Inc.***)

Bercik, Mark
    America's complete sports scholarship guide: (athletic and academic): a "how-to" guide to help you clearly understand the athletic recruiting process and how it leads to sports scholarships and financial aid! / by Mark Bercik
    p. cm.
    Includes bibliographical references and index.
    Audience: "For parents and student athletes (ages 8-18) of all sports."
    LCCN 2003091790
    ISBN 0-9721199-1-4

    1. Sports—Scholarships, fellowships, etc.—United States.
    2. Universities and colleges—United States—Admission—Planning.
    3. Athletes—Recruiting—United States—Handbooks, manuals, etc.
    4. Athletes—Education—United States. I. Title. II. Title: Sports scholarship guide

    GV351.B47 2003   796'.079'73
                                    QB103-200473

Dedicated to the memory

of

Michael S. Bercik

A man of quiet strength

from his son

Table of Contents

FOREWORD

John Delcos, New York Yankees' Beat Reporter,
    Gannett Westchester NY *Journal News* 12

Jerry Bonkowski, Former *USA Today* Sportswriter 13

What's Being Said about This Guide 14
Mission Statement 17
Who Is This Guide for? 19
Eight Reasons Student Athletes and Parents Need This Guide 21
Preview 23

PREGAME "WARM-UPS AND RULES"

Introduction 27
Topic Preview 28
Quick Tips/Learn the Rules! 30
Do You Know? 31
No Guarantees 33
What's a Variable? 34

INTRODUCTIONS

About the Author 39
Can I Get a Scholarship if I Play at a Small Town H.S.? 41
The Author's Recruiting Experience 42

INSPIRATIONAL STORIES "PEP TALK"

Don't Give up on Your Dreams 52

The Bobby Jones Story, Cleveland Browns', Buffalo Bills',
    and N. Y. Jets' Wide Receiver 54

The Ken Tirpack Story, Minnesota Twins' First Baseman, OSU All-American, and Indians' Scout 61

The Mike Barnett Story, Hitting Coach for Toronto Blue Jays 63

The Zack Walz Story, Arizona Cardinals' Linebacker, Dartmouth College All-American 68

ADVICE FROM "THE PROS"

Paul Maguire, TV Analyst for ESPN, Tight End for The Citadel 71

Solomon Wilcots, TV Football Analyst The *NFL on CBS*, Cornerback for Cincinnati Bengals, Minnesota Vikings, Pittsburgh Steelers, University of Colorado 74

Michael Zordich, Defensive Back for Philadelphia Eagles, Arizona Cardinals, New York Jets, Penn State All-American 78

Scott Knox, Pittsburgh Pirates' Free Agent Outfielder 82

Jeff Faine, Cleveland Browns' Center, Notre Dame All-American 85

Matt Wilhelm, San Diego Chargers' Linebacker, Ohio State All-American 86

Kelly Holcomb, Cleveland Browns' Quarterback, Middle Tennessee State University 89

Advice from Professional Scouts 90

ADVICE FROM "THE COACHES' CORNER"

Ron Stoops, Jr., High-school Football Coach from Famous College Coaching Family 93

Thom McDaniels, *USA Today*'s High-school Football Coach of the Year 97

John Zizzo, Colorado Rockies' Coach and Scout 113

Russ Hake, H.S. Football Coach, Murray State Halfback 116

Dan Deramo, Girls' High-school Volleyball Coach 121

HARD LUCK STORIES "THE REALITY OF SPORTS"

Marcus Marek, Ohio State All-American Linebacker,
    All-time OSU Career Tackling Leader 124

Andy Timko, University of Alabama Recruit,
    Baltimore Orioles' Shortstop 128

Jim Winterburn, High-school All-American Shortstop,
    Junior-high Track Coach 130

Al Gonzalez, High-school All-American Pitcher 133

Bill Sattler, Montreal Expos' Pitcher, H. S. Coach 135

Don Christian, Walk-on Pitcher, Tulane University 137

Todd Santore, Fresh out of College Baseball 141

ADVICE FROM "COUNSELORS AND ADVISORS"

Wayne Bair, High-school Guidance Counselor and Coach,
    MVP Infielder for Edinboro University 144

Dave Smercansky, H.S. Athletic Director, NCAA Pitching
    Champion, Youngstown State University 149

John Young, High-School Principal and Coach,
    Center for the University of Akron 152

Jeff Tarver, President of the Mentoring Student Athletes
    Foundation, Ohio State Free Safety 154

ADVICE FROM "PARENTS WITH EXPERIENCE"

Advice from Robert Marek, Father of an All-American Ohio State Linebacker 157

Advice from Milan Zordich, Father of a Penn State All-American and NFL Defensive Back 161

Advice from Andy Timko Sr., Father of an Alabama Recruit, 3rd - round Draft Pick, Baltimore Orioles 163

Advice from Ray Bowers, Father of NCAA All-time Leading Rusher R. J. Bowers, Grove City College 165

Advice from Don Watt, Father of 2001 Division I Baseball Scholarship Recruit 167

PROMOTE YOURSELF

College Coaches Offer Advice on Promoting Yourself 170
Recruiting Services—The Good, The Bad, The Ugly 176
Get Noticed at Camps 183
How to Promote Yourself 185
Communicating with College Coaches 187
College Sports Questionnaire Samples 189
Videotaping Angles and Tips 192
How to Find Valuable Contacts 205

ADVICE FROM "THE MEDIA"

Advice from Budd Bailey, Sports Department, *Buffalo News* 214

Advice from Greg Gulas, Sports Information Director, Former Head Baseball Coach, Youngstown State University 217

PARENTS' SECTION

Preparing Your Child for College Isn't an Easy Matter 221
Where Can You Find Out about Scholarships? 223

Advice from Walter Kohowski, Father of Division III
                                Football Recruit 224

Advice from Shirley Libeg, Mother of 2002 Division I
                                Baseball Scholarship Recruit 226

Advice from Financial Aid Advisors 228

NCAA ADVICE AND INFORMATION

Information from *2003-2004 NCAA Guide
                    for the College-bound Student-Athlete* 232

Academic Eligibility Requirements 233
Initial Eligibility Clearinghouse 239
Seven Points to Remember about Eligibility 240
NCAA Website Lists All Colleges and Universities 241
Recruiting 242
Questions You Should Ask 247
Scholarship Facts and Figures 251
What Are Your Chances of Hitting the Top? 253
National Letter of Intent 254
Which College Offers Which Sport? 255
What Is a "Seasonal Sport"? 256
NCAA Student Athlete Advisory Committee Info 257
Recruiting Terms 259

SUMMARY

Summary 264
Special Thanks 268
Index 270
How to Contact Us 272

10

FOREWORD

John Delcos,
New York Yankees' beat reporter,
Gannett Westchester, NY, *Journal News,*
says:

"The odds of a high-school athlete receiving a collegiate scholarship are small, and the odds of going on to play professional sports are even smaller.

"Let's face facts. Sports these days are about numbers, and while there's not a high-school athlete who hasn't for a moment gotten lost in the dream of the big time, whether it be the Rose Bowl, Final Four, or Super Bowl, less than one percent ever make it.

"There are so few Derek Jeters, Jason Kidds, and Tom Bradys in this world, and the few with that special talent don't need help. *America's Complete Sports Scholarship Guide* is for the rest. It emphasizes that the high-school student athlete's most important skill is not a jump shot or fast ball but an education.

"Mark Bercik, who has gone through the process himself, relates from personal experiences and those of others how to travel the academic/athletic road from high school to college. The most important thing he tells you is there are no shortcuts on that path. While recruiting services promise to make dreams come true, they don't have that power.

"*America's Complete Sports Scholarship Guide* empowers the student athlete with the knowledge of how to attract the attention of the university and informs the parents of what questions to ask the coach who comes into the living room.

"The competition is steep and knowledge is power, and *America's Complete Sports Scholarship Guide* provides that knowledge. It's a 'must' if playing collegiate sports is in your future or that of your son or daughter."

Jerry Bonkowski,
former *USA Today* sportswriter, says:

"Not every high school athlete is lucky enough to be a blue-chip prospect, bound for a Division I school on a full first-class scholarship ride. But those athletes who aren't need not give up hope. *Sports Scholarship Guide* is an outstanding reference and one of the most comprehensive sources to help college-bound athletes achieve their dreams within their means.

"When it comes to succeeding in sports, you need to know and be well-versed in the fundamentals. That's what Mark Bercik gives you—tips, suggestions, and coaching to help you not only get into college as an athlete but also how to pay for it once you get there and then to succeed both as a student and as an athlete.

"*SSG* is a grand slam of a book, covering all of the bases and giving college-bound athletes the information they need to know to make it both as students and athletes, academically and physically. If you're a high-school athlete who wants to take your game to the next level—to college, university, or junior college—*SSG* is the book that will help turn your dreams into reality."

"When it comes to student athletes winning the college recruiting and scholarship game, *Sports Scholarship Guide* is a grand slam, touchdown, and slam dunk all in one!"

What's Being Said about This Guide...

"The *Sports Scholarship Guide* was certainly helpful to my husband and me while we were going through the recruiting process with our son, who recently received a baseball scholarship to a Division I university."

**Shirley Libeg,
parent of a scholarship recipient from Ohio**

"This guide was great to have to refer to as my son was being recruited by various colleges across the country before finally deciding on accepting a Division I baseball scholarship."

**Gary Hinkson,
parent of a scholarship recipient from Pennsylvania**

"Very well constructed. Realistic advice from people who have been through the process. A must for every parent and high-school student athlete to help understand college participation."

**Jim Maughan,
athletic director, Ursuline High School, Youngstown, Ohio**

"Every high school student athlete, parent, and guidance department would do well to have a copy this guide."

**Steve Rohan,
high-school guidance counselor and girls' basketball coach**

"The recruiting process has changed dramatically in the last twenty years. Ballplayers in youth leagues, potential college prospects, and even the blue chip recruit will benefit from reading this guide."

**Gary DeNiro,
Parent and former linebacker,
University of Alabama, 1978-1979 National Champions**

"The *Sports Scholarship Guide* should be in the home of every young athlete, and on the desk of every high-school coach, guidance counselor, and principal in America.

"If playing sports in college is a goal or dream, then reading and re-reading this book is a must. It cuts through the fluff and misconceptions surrounding a very simple yet misunderstood process."

Tim Povtak,
***Orlando Sentinel* sportswriter and columnist**

The author and former Ohio University teammate, Mike Barnett (L), Toronto Blue Jays' hitting coach, prior to a Cleveland Indians game at Jacobs Fields in Cleveland, Ohio.

"You get only one chance at getting an athletic scholarship!

"The longer the student athlete and his/her parents take to understand the athletic scholarship process, the less likely the chances are of the student athlete ever obtaining an athletic and/or academic scholarship."

**Mike Barnett,
former University of Tennessee baseball coach,
major league hitting coach,
Toronto Blue Jays**

15

"Insight—valuable experience usually learned only from those who have been through the process. Covers all bases as far as those involved."

**Mike Florak,
head baseball coach,
Youngstown State University**

"Mark Bercik's publication is a 'must' for those athletes and students who believe a college scholarship is in their future, along with parents and youngsters who are participating in sports or excelling in their school work!

"This guide is just that—a guide for the many questions parents have concerning college offers. And it will save countless hours of searching for answers to those questions.

"If you're a parent of an athlete competing for a scholarship, you've got to read this guide."

**John "Cappy" Caparanis,
host of "Tip of the Cap"—award-winning sports talk show on
ESPN 1240 AM**

Mission Statement

It's never too early to begin planning for your college education and researching the possibilities of potential athletic and scholarship opportunities.

Our mission is to touch on every aspect involved in the collegiate athletic recruiting process. We will provide the necessary information you will need to realistically evaluate your athletic and academic talents.

Our goal is to make student athletes and their families aware of the fact that the chances of being recruited athletically are directly proportionate to their academic performance.

This information should help you decide which type of college is best suited for your athletic and academic abilities.

"The *Sports Scholarship Guide* is a high-school coach's best friend!

"Not only does it provide realistic information on the recruiting process for student athletes and parents, but it is also an excellent resource guide for high-school coaches to refer to."

**Jim Vivo,
head football coach,
Youngstown Ursuline High School,
the 2000 Ohio state champions**

Who Is This Guide for?

Student Athletes

- high-school athletes
- junior-high athletes
- college walk-ons
- college transfers

Parents

To help them understand the importance of academic scholarships and why they can become a very instrumental factor when it comes to recruiting for coaches of sports who have limited recruiting budgets.

If you were a college coach on a tight budget and you had to decide between the two prospects listed below, with all of the athletic factors involved being equal, which prospect would you choose?

	Prospect 1	Prospect 2
grade point average (GPA)	3.5	3.0
rank in senior class	20 of 200 (10%)	60 of 200 (30%)
number of academic scholarships awarded	5	2
potential value of academic scholarships	$8,000	$4,000

This is a "no brainer" for a college recruiter. Sometimes at certain colleges, the better athlete will be overlooked for financial reasons, whether it's fair or not.

High-school Guidance Counselors and Coaches

Great informational tool to help answer questions on athletic recruiting and college scholarships from student athletes and their parents.

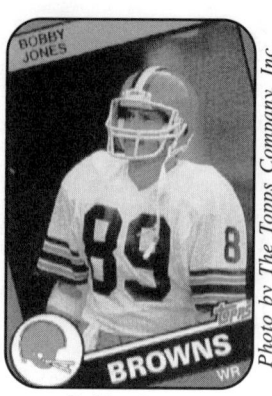

Photo by The Topps Company, Inc.

Bobby Jones

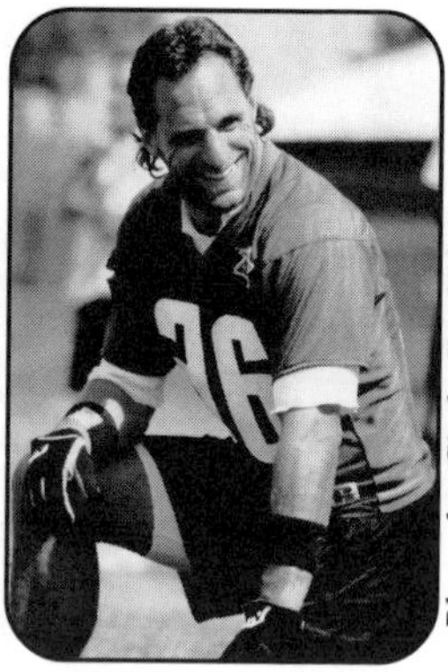
Photo by Cindy Zordich

Michael Zordich

Photo by Bob Knott

Solomon Wilcots

Matt Wilhelm

Photo by Marc Jablonski

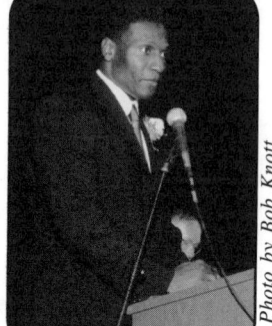

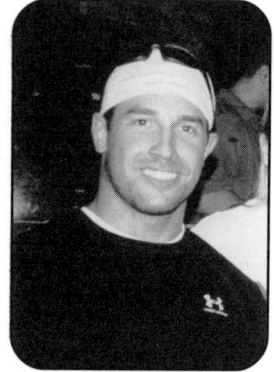

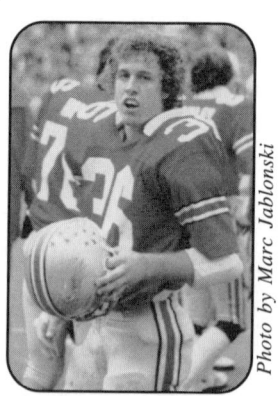

Marcus Marek

"This guide will certainly be helpful to young athletes and their parents.

"It is refreshing to see how the author and all of the people interviewed are giving something back to the game to help young athletes understand the recruiting process and the importance of having a college education."

Joe Carbone,
head baseball coach,
Ohio University

Eight Reasons Student Athletes and Parents Need This Guide

1. *To learn the rules.* If you don't follow the rules and meet the requirements, you won't be eligible to play.

2. *To clearly understand* all of the factors involved in the complex and competitive athletic recruiting process.

3. *To learn how to communicate* with current and former coaches, athletes, scouts, and alumni.

4. *To become realistic* when deciding which colleges are best suited for your athletic and academic abilities.

5. *To develop a marketing plan* to promote yourself.

6. *To know the benefits and differences* among NCAA division levels I, II, and III; and junior colleges.

7. *To find information on academic scholarships*: where to look, when to apply; etc.

8. *To discover information on websites* about tuition costs, courses and majors offered, enrollment, graduation rates, male-to-female ratios, and whatever else you need to know about any particular college.

There is no exact formula for obtaining an athletic scholarship, but once you have read this guide, you will be able to figure out your most realistic and sensible chances of getting an athletic and/or academic scholarship.

"Reality for players and parents—this guide should be read by all players who aspire to compete at the next level."

**Ed Stacey,
former Texas A&M graduate assistant coach,
associate scout for the New York Yankees**

Preview

This guide is about **reality**!

It also could have been titled *Life's Lessons*. We hope that it will take you beyond the scope of just the athletic recruiting process that leads to sports scholarships. You need to realize that a scholarship doesn't come looking for you. Unless you're a blue chip recruit who's dominating in a sport, you'll have to learn how to search for scholarships and then earn one by selling yourself.

This guide was written to educate and prepare parents and students who are serious about playing sports in college. If you think it's easy to get an athletic scholarship, then you definitely need to read this guide. If you're aware of how difficult it is to get an athletic scholarship, then you're heading in the right direction. *Half of knowledge is knowing where to find it.* If you're reading this guide, you're halfway there, and the rest is up to you!

There are many real-life inspirational and hard-luck stories in this guide that you may find hard to believe. What you'll find even harder to believe is that many stories similar to these exist in the area in which you live and in every area clear across the U. S. Just ask anybody in your area about its sports history.

You'll get a good idea of how unique each athletic recruiting experience can be. *There is no exact formula for getting an athletic scholarship.* The information in this guide will help you understand the recruiting process and collegiate sports. It also will give you the expertise to ask the right questions and seek valuable help as you pursue an athletic scholarship.

"*The Sports Scholarship Guide* educates and prepares parents and high-school athletes about the realities of high-school, collegiate, and professional sports....It will help young athletes of all ages understand how they need to conduct themselves on and off the field to even be considered a prospect."

**Mike Nittoli,
parent and San Francisco, CA, youth league coach,
former Chicago White Sox catcher**

PREGAME "WARM-UPS AND RULES"

Photo by Marc Jablonski

26

Introduction

You, too, can be successful at playing sports in college and getting an athletic scholarship. We're going to show you and your parents what you need to know about the collegiate athletic recruiting process that leads to sports scholarships. This guide will benefit parents and student athletes (ages 8-18) of all men and women's sports.

We'll show you how to sell yourself as a knowledgeable and mature student athlete to the college recruiters who award these scholarships. You'll learn the skills and develop confidence to be able to speak to these decision makers in a comfortable and professional manner. You'll learn how to get yourself noticed, find valuable contacts, and effectively promote yourself as an attractive recruit.

A diverse selection of the book focuses on real-life stories and advice from athletes in all walks of life. These folks want "to give something back to the game" and provide a variety of their experiences and advice on the recruiting process and subsequent college and later life experiences. They have a common theme: Get your college education and diploma!

You and your parents will learn that awarding scholarships is a business and that you are seen through the eyes of a college coach as an "investment." We'll show you how to sell yourself as a good investment to these college recruiters.

For the first time, all of the necessary information on the athletic recruiting process and sports scholarships in the *real* world are under one cover, and that book is in your hands.

Many student athletes have achieved their dream of playing sports in college through an athletic scholarship, and many more will continue to achieve this every year. And the dream *can* be good. It's worked for us, and after you finish reading this guide, we hope it will work for you. Read on!

Topic Preview

PREGAME "WARM-UP AND RULES"

This chapter asks questions that you may never have asked before, along with giving much food for thought about "guarantees" and "variables."

INTRODUCTIONS

The author, Mark Bercik, talks about his own sports recruiting experience and whether it's possible to get a scholarship if you play at a small high school.

INSPIRATIONAL STORIES "PEP TALK"

Real-life stories and advice from professional athletes and coaches who never gave up on their dreams.

ADVICE FROM "THE PROS"

This chapter includes interviews and advice from former and current professional athletes and scouts.

ADVICE FROM "THE COACHES' CORNER"

This chapter includes interviews and advice from former and current high-school, college, and professional coaches who are well respected across the country.

HARD-LUCK STORIES, "THE REALITY OF SPORTS"

This chapter deals with the reality of sports. It includes advice from former great athletes who tell why they weren't able to make it to the next level.

ADVICE FROM "COUNSELORS AND ADVISORS"

Former college athletes who are now counselors and advisors share their knowledge and experience on today's athletic recruiting process that leads to scholarships and financial aid.

ADVICE FROM "PARENTS WITH EXPERIENCE"

Parents who have gone through the recruiting process with their children first-hand provide valuable information for both parents and student athletes.

PROMOTE YOURSELF

In this chapter, you'll learn what colleges coaches are looking for in a recruit and how to go about selling yourself to these recruiters, how to avoid bad recruiting services, and how to have yourself video taped to show your capabilities to your best advantage.

ADVICE FROM "THE MEDIA"

Advice from the media covers both high-school and college sports.

PARENTS' SECTION

Read tips on where to find out about scholarships, how to avoid scholarship scams, which websites have a wealth of information, and more advice from parents with experience.

NCAA ADVICE AND INFORMATION

Don't blow this section off! It's only the tip of the iceberg as far as all of the information that the NCAA provides, as well as extremely helpful info provided by the Student Athlete Advisory Committee that consists of college student athletes. If you're serious about college athletics, this chapter is a "must."

Quick Tips

The one common bit of advice that everybody who is or has been involved in the recruiting process should tell you is that you should go to college, first and foremost, to get your education. If anybody tells you otherwise, we strongly suggest that you ask their reasoning.

The only possible exception is if you're offered a professional contract right out of high school. In that case, you should have your college education paid for and included in your contract before you even consider signing a contract.

If that professional organization doesn't agree to do so, then perhaps you should consider your other options. If they're not willing to pay for your education while you're sacrificing your time and hard work for their team, then probably you aren't as valuable a prospect to their organization as they may lead you to believe.

Learn the Rules!

If you don't follow the rules—you don't play! (You've worked too hard to be ineligible.)

If you still don't understand the rules after reading this guide, contact the NCAA (National Collegiate Athletic Association) at 317/917-6222 or visit their extensive and detailed website at www.ncaa.org.

Your guidance counselor, coach, or athletic director should provide you with *the NCAA Guide for the College Bound Student Athlete*, which is free.

Do You Know?

Do you know...

1. that regardless of how great an athlete you may be, if you don't meet the NCAA academic and eligibility requirements, *you don't play?* You have to be approved by the NCAA Clearinghouse each year for Divisions I and II.

2. what the academic eligibility requirements are?

3. in what high-school grade your accumulative grade point average begins to count?

4. the total number of official and unofficial college visits you're allowed?

5. in what high-school school grade coaches start tracking prospects?

6. where to find out about available academic scholarships?

7. that approximately 1.5 million senior student athletes are eligible for athletic and academic scholarships each spring?

8. that the chances of receiving an athletic scholarship are about one in 100 (one percent)?

9. that the chances of receiving an academic scholarship are totally up to you? Approximately four out of ten students receive academic financial assistance.

10. that academic scholarships are awarded on a first-come, first-served basis? The earlier in the year that you apply, the more aid you're likely to receive.

No Guarantees

We can't guarantee that you will receive an athletic scholarship if you read this guide.

There's no exact formula or magical answer to obtaining an athletic scholarship.

It all depends on

1. whether or not you realize that a scholarship doesn't come looking for you;
2. how hard you work at your sport and finding credible contacts who can recommend you;
3. how much you research your top choices of colleges that you want to attend;
4. whether you're choosing the right situation for your athletic talent level, size, and speed;
5. whether the colleges you choose are recruiting your position;
6. whether you're able to play several positions;
7. whether your style of play matches the style of play at the college you're interested in;
8. whether you can create opportunities to be seen by college recruiters; *and most important of all:*
9. how well you perform and how you carry yourself when you have the chances to show your talents.

Editor's note: *How you handle and respond to your mistakes during a game is just as important as performing well. Coaches want to see how maturely you react to failure.*

Guarantees

We can guarantee that you'll find this guide informative, inspiring, and useful

1. after you read this guide, you'll be thinking about your future realistically, academically, financially, and sensibly;

2. the more you learn and understand about the entire athletic recruiting process, the more you'll learn about yourself and the more help you'll receive from your parents, coaches, teachers, and guidance counselors; and

3. you'll consider having a Plan B in case things don't work out well for you athletically.

What are you going to do if you're injured or overlooked and you never get a scholarship?

What if you don't want to give up on your dreams or goals and the only chance you have is to walk on at a college, but your family isn't able to come up with the money for you to attend? Now what do you do? Any type of academic financial aid would surely come in handy here.

We can guarantee that you could save thousands of dollars if you read this guide. You don't need to get a 4.0 GPA to get academic assistance. There are many nonathletic scholarships available that you may qualify for if you know where to look and who to ask. *Information is power!*

What's a "Variable"?

The only possible way for you to clearly understand the athletic recruiting process is to learn the meaning of the word "variable": *1. apt or likely to change or vary; changeable, inconstant, fickle, fluctuating, etc., and 2. that which can be changed or varied.*

There are so many variables involved with the athletic recruiting process that you can easily be overwhelmed to the point of having sleepless nights, trying to weigh all of the options while trying to make the right decision. If it helps you at all, this behavior is common; just ask student athletes and parents who've experienced this adventure.

You're going to have to educate yourself on this process. This guide is exactly what it's called: *a guide.* Both you (the student athlete), and your parents are going to have to

- learn what questions to ask about recruiting,

- ask as many people as you can about their experiences and for their advice,

- figure out what's the best situation for your athletic and academic abilities,

- come up with a marketing game plan on how you're going to promote yourself to the top colleges of your choice—more efficiently than your competition, and

- absolutely have a back-up plan—Plan B. This is where your academics (GPA, SAT, and ACT) play a major role, especially at Division III level, where athletic scholarships are not awarded.

The best way to explain variables to you and for you to learn from and understand how often they arise is by showing you how frequently they appear in a recruiting experience. On the other hand, you also should note that different people answer differently, according to their knowledge, experience, and expectations. For example, I'll share my personal experience with you, as will other athletes, allowing you to notice the variables.

I strongly suggest you and your parents learn not only how to ask, but also what kind of questions to ask, people who've been through the recruiting experience. Here are the most common ones.

1. What advice do you have for high school student athletes?

2. What advice do you have for their parents?

3. What advice do you have for junior-high athletes?

4. What do college coaches look for when recruiting student athletes?

5. What do you suggest that student athletes do to get themselves noticed and promote themselves?

6. How did you get noticed?

7. Describe your collegiate athletic recruiting experience.

8. What was your decision based on?

9. Would you do anything differently if you had the chance to do it again?

10. Who were the most instrumental individuals in your situation?

11. What are the most important factors you believe that student athletes should be aware of in the transition from high school to the collegiate sports level?

12. What's your opinion on attending sports camps?

13. What do you suggest is the best way for student athletes to find out what division level is best suited for their athletic and academic abilities?

14. What are some of the negative factors that would immediately turn a college coach away from recruiting a student athlete, regardless of how talented he/she may be?

15. Do you feel a student athlete's chances of being recruited would increase if college coaches know that he/she will receive academic money for college because of good grades?

While many other questions are certainly worth asking, you'll see where these questions lead as you read the following interviews. Using these questions initially in your own situations will give you a good base on which to make decisions. *Information is power!*

INTRODUCTIONS

Mark Bercik (sitting) introduces a parent and his son, who played for the Line Drive Baseball Academy team that Bercik managed, to his former Ohio University teammate, Mike Barnett, the Toronto Blue Jays' hitting coach, prior to a Cleveland Indians' ball game at Jacobs field, Cleveland, Ohio.

The author poses for a picture at an Easter Seals fund-raising banquet in Youngstown, Ohio with Archie Griffin, Associate Athletic Director at Ohio State and the only two-time Heisman Trophy winner.

Coach Bercik (standing far right) with his 15-16-year-old Line Drive Baseball Academy team that finished in 9th-place in the country in the Mickey Mantle Regional Baseball Tournament in Cincinnati, Ohio.

About the Author

Mark Bercik has been involved in the athletic recruiting process in some capacity since 1975 when he was a 15-year-old junior shortstop who began receiving letters from colleges and advice from professional scouts. He attended a high school in Brookfield, Ohio, a small town of nearly 10,000, with a graduating class of slightly over 100 students. Brookfield is located on the Ohio/Pennsylvania border in the middle of the nationally known and tradition-rich sports communities of Northeastern Ohio and Western Pennsylvania. This area is an athletic recruiting hotbed for college coaches who recruit high schools for all sports in Ohio's Cleveland, Youngstown/Warren, and Akron/Canton/Massillon areas and Pennsylvania's Pittsburgh/Beaver Falls/Sharon/Farrell areas.

He credits his coaches and his family's upbringing for being able to get a college baseball scholarship—especially his father. His dad coached him from the age of 10 when he started playing baseball until he was 15.

In the fall of his 16th year, Mark received a Division I scholarship and signed a Letter of Intent to play baseball at Ohio University, Athens, Ohio, where he was a member of the Mid-American Conference team, as well as MVP and captain of his team. His goal was to play pro baseball, which he did later in Washington and Utah. To date, Mark is still among the youngest athletes ever to receive an athletic scholarship at 16.

In his professional career, the author has been in direct contact with thousands of high school, collegiate, and professional coaches on many levels as a player, coach, and scout. He worked as a personal assistant to Woody Kern, the owner of minor league teams in New York, Washington, North Carolina, and California.

His experience includes developing relationships with university and pro sports coaches, as well as being the owner/operator of Tiger Fitness Products, a manufacturer of weight equipment that designed and set up weight rooms in sports facilities, such as at Duke University.

While he ran his business in Athens, Ohio, Mark organized a fund-raising promotion on the campus of Ohio University to benefit a scholarship fund for future university athletes in Tiger Fitness Products' name. In addition to being an author and running America Sports Publishing, which provides sports-related books for junior-high and high-school athletes, their parents, coaches, and guidance counselors, Mark also helps youngsters of all ages as a personal instructor and coach for the Line-Drive Baseball Academy in Youngstown, Ohio.

He decided to write this sports scholarship guide because of all the uncertainties and misconceptions that student athletes and parents/guardians have about the athletic recruiting process. He also wanted to stress the importance of having a college education to fall back on when the student athlete's playing days are over.

"There are so many factors involved in collegiate sports and the business side of recruiting that student athletes and parents/guardians aren't aware of, so I felt there was a need for this kind of guide," Mark says.

"I was very fortunate to have obtained an enormous amount of knowledge through my own personal experiences and those of my fellow high school, college, and professional teammates and coaches. I feel that at this point in my life that writing this book to benefit today's student athletes is something I was put on this earth to do—my way of 'giving something back to the game' so to speak." Bercik said.

Below is the small town high-school basketball team the author played on that had eight players involved in college sports, with five receiving Division I athletic scholarships.

Kneeling: Dave Bock, John Lott (University of Michigan), Jeff Tarver (Ohio State), Mark Bercik (Ohio University), Standing: John Leiphiemer (Mount Union), Darwin Ulmer (University of Arizona), Marcus Marek (Ohio State), Pete Durman, Frank Sees, Gary Sabulski (Walsh College), Ed Pryts (Penn State).

Can I Get a Scholarship if I Play at a Small High School?

Mark says, "Although I'll never claim to be a recruiting "expert" (I'll leave that title to the current college coaches), I can speak proudly and honestly about how it's very possible to get noticed and recruited from a small town. I just don't buy the idea that 'I'm from a small town; I'll never be recruited.'"

Within a five-year period in a small town where I went to high school, an incredible number of fellow classmates went on to colleges on athletic scholarships; three became All-Americans. A remarkable total of six classmates from this small school went on to play sports on a professional level. We had eight athletes from our high-school basketball team in my junior year who played sports in college; five of them received Division I scholarships.

Some classmates went to major Division I schools, such as Ohio State, Penn State, Michigan, Arizona, West Virginia, Pittsburgh, and Notre Dame, while others went to Southern Illinois, Miami of Ohio, Kent State, Allegheny, Clarion, Hiram, Walsh, Lakeland, Mount Union, Ohio Wesleyan, and Youngstown State. Scholarships were awarded in football, basketball, baseball, track, golf, and wrestling.

One of those, Marcus Marek, was a two-time All-American linebacker who became the all-time record holder for tackles in a career at Ohio State. One was Ed Pryts, an All-American linebacker at Penn State the very same year, and another Tom Volarich, became a NAIA Division II All-American in basketball at Malone College.

Another athlete from my home town, Bobby Jones, was basically overlooked as a wide receiver by college coaches and ended up playing for seven years in the NFL as a wide receiver—he never played collegiate sports! (Read more about him in the next chapter.)

Later in this guide, you'll read about experiences and advice on recruiting from many of these individuals and their coaches.

The Author's Recruiting Experience

My story seems long, but my experience was actually short and sweet. Let's hope your recruiting experience will be as good.

Q: Describe your recruiting experience

A: As a baseball player in my junior year (age 15), I started receiving questionnaires from small schools (Division II and III) that were within my state of Ohio or only hours away in neighboring states. I looked at the brochures and letters several times a day for the first month. After a good high-school junior year and summer league season, I started getting questionnaires from Division I schools from Ohio, nearby Pennsylvania and Michigan, and even as far away as the University of Miami, Florida. I can't believe that to this day; how did such a major program from such a distance hear about somebody like me? *(Somebody liked me!)* By the time I made my decision in the Fall of my senior year, I had over 20 schools contact me. However, I was interested in only two of those schools at that time, and I ended up visiting only one. *But I never burned a bridge with any college, regardless of how small it was.*

I distinctly remember talking to one coach from a very small Division III college who seemed to call every week even though I told him honestly that I was pretty sure I knew I was going to a Division I school. But I let him know that I'd certainly remember his interest in me. (I was thinking: What if I get injured again and the Division I schools lose interest in me?)

Q: How were you noticed?

A: I played my second season of summer ball in a very competitive league that was a half-hour from home. This league received a lot of exposure, and doing well meant that your name would be heard by college coaches, which is exactly what happened. In my case, an opposing team had a freshman player at Ohio University. Both this player and the coach of the opposing summer league team mentioned my name to the Ohio University coach.

The opposing coach wrote a letter on my behalf to this coach, which I didn't know about till later on. This college coach came to a high-quality tournament where he could watch over 20 different teams play throughout the week. He came to say "Hi" and watch his player from Ohio U., as well as future prospects. I happened to be picked as an all-star by this same team for this tournament; I had a good game the first day and also the second. Many other college coaches and scouts attended this tournament and sent me letters in the fall of my senior year.

Q: **Who were the individuals most instrumental in your recruiting adventure?**

A: Without a doubt, my father was most instrumental— he had the insight to know where I needed to be playing to get noticed. He never made me do anything I didn't want to do as far as baseball goes. When I was 15, he asked me if I really was serious about baseball and if I wanted to progress in the game. He knew I was, but he always asked the question to make it my decision, not his. For you parents out there: This is a very important point to remember.

The author's father, Michael (third from left), sitting with Pony League championship trophy in front of him.

My father asked questions of other parents and athletes and found out what a parent should know about the recruiting process, both athletically and academically, well before the time ever came where I was allowed to be recruited. He never made a phone call or sent a letter to any colleges because he had the insight to know that I needed to be seen playing the game at an early age. *This was our marketing game plan: Play against the best competition available.* The rest was up to me to perform well, which I did, and everything fell into place; I was noticed. The key is to get noticed before your junior year, if possible; the sooner your name gets heard, the better, Ideally, you want to be receiving questionnaires from colleges by your junior year; don't be discouraged if you're not. This just means you've got some catching up do to with your competition. This is where sports camps, tryouts, showcases, and tournaments come into play.

Q: What was your decision, and what was it based on?

A: As with every recruit's decision, mine was also unique. Both my dad and I assessed the entire situation and concluded that athletically, I should commit as early as possible to my choice of colleges while they were interested. Keep this in mind: *If you don't accept a scholarship when it's offered, it just might not still be there when you're ready to decide. Not all coaches have the patience to wait for you to decide because they have other recruits in mind.*

There were two main reasons for this thinking.

1. I had fractured both of my feet at the start of the basketball season my junior year and fractured a foot right before my baseball season. Why risk getting hurt and losing scholarships? This is something to consider very strongly if you decide to sign early. Colleges can withdraw their offers if they know you're damaged goods. (I never volunteered the fact that I had broken my feet to any of the colleges that contacted me.)

2. We figured, for specific reasons, that there wasn't much to gain and possibly a lot to lose by waiting for a college to come watch me play during my high school season.

   A: The college and high school seasons are played at the same time, and even if a college planned to watch me play, the game could be postponed because of the Northeast Ohio weather. And our baseball program was nothing to speak of, especially since the baseball field was the parking lot for the football games. You can imagine how much fun it was to be an infielder there! (For the record, we played 11 games that season.)

B: I had no idea who was going to be my baseball coach the upcoming season.

I narrowed my decision to Ohio University and Miami of Florida. Miami University, an annual national power, invited me to visit. They couldn't offer a scholarship until they could see me play, but from what they'd heard about me, they were more than willing to invite me to walk on. The coach I talked to was Skip Bertman, who seemed to be a great guy and was a great motivator. Coach Bertman later went on to be the head coach at Louisiana State University and has five national championships to his credit.

Bercik tags out runner for the University of South Carolina.

I visited Ohio U. first and came out very satisfied with the many factors that should be involved in anyone's decision, regardless of whether a decision is made early or not. It really turned out to be an easy decision even though I would have loved to play in Florida for one of the best teams in the country. I just couldn't expect my parents to pay for me to go to college if it had come down to that, which I'm fairly sure it would have, at least for my first year, when another perfectly good college was willing to pay for my education.

1. I loved the campus, the type of students who attended, the activities available for students, and all of the academic courses that were offered.

2. I liked the fact that they made me aware that baseball would likely be only about ten percent of my entire life even though I'd attend on an athletic scholarship and especially that I shouldn't plan to go to college just to play baseball.

3. I knew a student who also happened to be a junior on the baseball team. (Knowing someone on campus when you move away from home for the first time is always a major relief and something to consider when making your choice.) Recruiting coaches want to know if you know anybody at their college and will try to arrange for you to see that individual while you are there to make you more comfortable.

4. Former coach Bob Wren developed a great program and tradition. At that time, Hall of Famer Mike Schmidt was an all-star third-baseman in the majors, along with Arizona Diamondbacks' manager Bob Brenly.

5. The team always played several nationally ranked teams on its spring trip down South and played in a very competitive conference where it appeared that three to four players were signed annually to professional contracts.

6. The coach's (Jerry France) philosophy was very down-to-earth. From what I'd heard and seen, he was the type you could trust and who would allow you freedom to grow as a player and as a person. If you made mistakes in life, you should grow from them, just like in baseball. (You can be a good hitter in baseball and fail seven out of ten times—you need to learn how to handle failure as well as success. You don't want to have peaks and valleys in your sport or in your life; you need to be on an even plane right in the middle of the peaks and valleys.)

7. Even though it would be my decision, it helped that my parents liked the coach and the school. (Athletes: Ask your parents or guardians what they think and why; appreciate their input. Normally, there's nobody else who cares about you as much as they do.)

Q: Would you do anything different if you had the chance to do it again?

A: As far as my choice of Ohio University, *no*! As far as my decisions while I was in college, *yes*! I would have gone to see my academic advisors when I was supposed to as soon as I arrived in my freshman year and many more times throughout my education time. I enrolled in classes that were way out of my league for a freshman. I thought I knew everything at that time of my life—I learned the hard way.

Take my advice and that of many others: *Thoroughly understand what classes you're taking your first semester in college; not every student is prepared properly for the transition from high school to the college atmosphere!* I've seen many people who quit college after just one quarter or semester because they were overwhelmed by their first impression of college.

As I grow older, I recognize all of the mistakes I made in my life, academically and personally. When I was in college, all I really wanted to do was to play ball, party, sleep, eat, and then study—in that order. I've been out of college for 20 years and don't have a degree even though I attended college for four years. I left to play pro baseball and planned to finish later, but I never did. I realize now that my priorities were in the wrong order. That's why in retrospect, I'm telling young people today how important it is to get an education and a degree. Don't make the same mistake I did. Stick with school until you have that degree in your hand!

Bercik hits against the University of Florida

Q: Do you have any advice for high school athletes who will soon be college freshmen?

A: Form a team with your parents or guardians where you can openly discuss all the variables involved in the recruiting process — athletics academics, and finances. *You need to understand how much money*

47

it costs to go to college and appreciate the fact that your parents or guardians will more than likely be footing the bill or at least part of it.

Sure, an athletic scholarship would be nice, but you can help both yourself and your parents by becoming eligible for numerous scholarships that are available based on grades. You'll learn later in this guide just how academic scholarships can help you get yourself recruited athletically.

This may sound odd at first, but you need to display good sportsmanship at all times! You need to keep in mind that opposing coaches pick all-star teams, and they're asked by college coaches which are the better players they've faced. There may not be a better reference than an opposing coach—remember that! Even opposing players, when sent questionnaires, are asked about the top players they've played against. Sometimes you have to bite your lip for your own good.

An unbelievable example of how important it is to be liked by coaches is what happened during my freshman year in college. I played behind a third-baseman named Scott Kuvinka at Ohio University. For some unknown reason, the opposing coaches who voted in the Mid-American Conference selected Scott as the third best third-baseman in our league. The *Sporting News* magazine named Scott as the best third-baseman in the entire country, and the Pittsburgh Pirates selected him in the third round of the baseball draft only weeks later. The point is that coaches don't always select the most talented opposing player; they select the opposing player whom they like the most!

Q: What advice do you have for junior-high athletes?

A: Be prepared academically; have good study habits in order. Remember that your GPA covers your grades from grades 9-12. Otherwise, learn the fundamentals of whatever sport you participate in and enjoy the sport and the competition that goes with it. You have plenty of time to develop physically, so stay ahead of the game academically now. Find out during these years if you really DO love playing a sport. Get out of the house; go outside and be active!

Q: What's your opinion on sports camps?

A: Every student athlete needs to attend a sports camp at some period in his/her young life. Camps where you stay for several days to a week are excellent for the athlete to get a taste of what it's like to be independent and learn social skills on top of athletic instruction. (I dreaded going away to a basketball camp for a week when I was 13, but I can tell you it was a very worthwhile experience even if I didn't like it at the time.) *I can't think of a better way to be noticed and get advice than at a college camp.* If you're really interested in a particular college, you can't beat talking to the coach at a camp, seeing the campus, receiving professional instruction, and showing your skills to the coach. (One of the biggest mistakes young athletes make is to attempt to contact or play at colleges where their athletic or academic talent levels don't match the college's expectations.)

You can ask the college coach if he thinks you have what it takes to play at that particular level. If he says yes, that's great. If he says something other than yes, he's probably being polite. No big deal, just go to Plan B even if it's at a lower level. More than likely, you'll be happier participating at the Division II or Division III level than maybe sitting the bench at Division I.

Q: Do you think you need to know someone or get a break to get an athletic scholarship?

A: Yes—I would say that 99 percent of the time, you need somebody's help, guidance, or advice. You need to figure out how to create your own breaks yourself where you have an opportunity to be seen by college recruiters. Your break could be a person connected to a college or even a coach. The only exception would be if you are a phenomenal (Blue Chip) athlete. Even then you'll need to be open for advice in selecting which college to attend. In my experience, it was actually an opposing coach and player who promoted me.

Besides my family's guidance and advice, I was blessed with having some special coaches and people in my life. You can learn as much, if not more, from coaches of sports other than the one you play. I consider this a break.

Coach John Cullen, our basketball coach in junior and senior high, was a coach who helped us understand at a young age the whole picture of attending college—not just playing sports but also the importance of receiving an education. He had the ability to make sports fun; he even made conditioning as fun as possible. He taught me the importance of being a team player and a leader, as well as sportsmanship. These three qualities directly resulted in my getting a scholarship, being captain and MVP of my college baseball team, and being named a member of the All-Conference team.

Our high school football coach, John Delserone, was very instrumental in organizing a baseball conditioning program for me. I never even played football for him! He was a special man who saw the desire I had to be the best baseball player I could be. One day in the weight room, he asked me how baseball players train for their sport. I didn't answer, and he said, "You don't know, do you?" When I said, "No," he said, "Get your butt in my office—we're going to find out."

He asked who I thought was the best college team in the country, and I answered, "Either Arizona or Arizona State."

"Well, we're going to call them both," he said and called both coaches right there in front of me and took notes the entire time. Coach Delserone was not one of my teachers, a baseball player or baseball coach, and yet he made those phone calls for me because he knew I had the desire. To this day, I pass on to the players I coach the advice I picked up that day.

Both of those coaches had the ability to read my mind, and I was lucky! You young athletes can't rely on coaches reading your minds, though. You have to let them know your dreams and goals and show them you're serious. Ask them for advice and don't think you know more than they do because *you don't!*

The bottom line is that coaches and former athletes will help you. It's a natural and rewarding thing for us to do, but we really want to help youngsters who are serious and appreciative.

All of my baseball coaches had a positive influence that helped me be successful. Many other players and coaches helped me, and I can't write about all of them, but I'd like to thank them all right now. I'm sure that my athletic career wouldn't have turned out so positive without their knowledge and guidance along the way. *Information is power!*

INSPIRATIONAL STORIES

"PEP TALK"

Don't Give Up on Your Dreams!

What if the following athletes gave up on their dreams because they didn't receive the exposure and recognition they deserved? They happened to be overlooked and might have been passed over entirely if not for some special coaches who could see the talent they possessed.

- Barry Sanders, Detroit Lions—only two scholarship offers

- Jerry Rice, San Francisco 49ers—one small college offer

- John Stockton, Utah Jazz—one scholarship offer to Gonzaga University

- Michael Jordan, Chicago Bulls—didn't make the varsity basketball team in his sophomore year in high-school.

- Scottie Pippen, Chicago Bulls—not heavily recruited; played basketball at NCAA Division II school Central Arkansas

- Andre Reed, Buffalo Bills—played football at Division II Kutztown University

- Kirby Puckett, Minnesota Twins—played football at Triton Junior College; signed as a baseball player

Each of these athletes will eventually become a "Hall of Famer" in his respective sport.

There may be only a small number of successful stories of athletes of this caliber, but there are also numerous other athletes who, for whatever reason, weren't heavily recruited but refused to give up on their dreams and went on to have successful careers.

These next athletes, too, were passed by in the recruiting area but went on to make their names known.

- London Fletcher, St. Louis Rams, linebacker—played basketball at Gannon University before transferring to Division III John Carroll University to play football at a small school with an enrollment of only 3,600

- Mike Piazza, New York Mets, catcher—61st- round draft pick in baseball draft

- Bobby Jones, former NFL wide receiver for seven years—one of a handful of athletes to ever play in the NFL without participating in collegiate sports

- Spud Webb, at only 5'7" and 145 lbs, still made it to the NBA. He says, "If you don't believe in yourself, nobody else will."

- Jeff Garcia, quarterback for the San Francisco 49ers, received no scholarship offers out of high school. He walked on at a junior college before he transferred to San Jose State University.

- Jason Giambi, first baseman for the New York Yankees, and Jeremy Shockey, 1st-round draft pick for the New York Giants in 2002, were not offered scholarships out of high school. They both had to walk on and make the team before they eventually were offered athletic scholarships to Long Beach State and the University of Miami, respectively.

- Five athletes from either Division II or III colleges were on the Denver Broncos' 1999 Super Bowl championship team

Author's note: *For you young athletes who aspire to become a coach, one of my teammates at Ohio University, Mike Barnett, was a walk-on and a back-up catcher who never received any scholarship money. But he never gave up on his dreams and is now a major league hitting coach for the Toronto Blue Jays.*

The Bobby Jones Story, Former NFL Player

Bobby, a former athlete from Brookfield High School in Ohio (the author's high school), was a wide receiver and defensive back in high school. He received only a few invitations to attend some small colleges. When he went to camp, they wanted him to play only defensive back. He wanted to play wide receiver, so he left college before his freshman season even began.

Four years later, he attended a tryout for the New York Jets and made the team as a wide receiver, where he played for five seasons and then one season each for the Cleveland Browns and the Buffalo Bills.

The author interviewed this gutsy player who was overlooked by every college coach in the country as a wide receiver but continued to believe in himself and made it all the way to the NFL *by never giving up on his dreams!*

Q: Describe your recruiting experience.

A: I had three different experiences with recruiting: two as a football player and one as a basketball player. Each of these schools was on a different level; two offered scholarships and the other financial aid.

All three were after me pretty hard. It was a fulfilling experience in that it made a young athlete realize his childhood dreams of playing sports in college might happen. Being wanted is very exciting—coaches and universities welcoming me with open arms, trying to sell me on their school.

My experiences were not overwhelming like some highly recruited athletes. So I would say my recruiting experience was a positive and exciting one.

Q: How were you noticed?

A: I was noticed in high school. Two universities were sent films of some of my games, and also, schools were interested to see more of me because coaches I'd played for in high school wrote letters and made phone calls of recommendation.

Q: Who were the individuals most instrumental in your recruiting adventure?

A: For the recruiting opportunity, it would have to be my high-school coaches—they got the whole thing started. Being at a small high school with not very good programs at the time made it hard to be noticed. So if not for their help, I'm not sure that it would have been possible.

Once the recruiting process began, my contact was primarily with the head coaches and position coaches of the university.

Q: What was your decision and what was it based on?

A: Two schools wanted me to play football, and the other wanted me as a basketball player. Initially, I'd signed with the school that wanted me for my basketball ability. I felt at that time that my first love was basketball after saying "no" to the two schools who wanted me for football, one of which had offered a full scholarship.

I was very satisfied and excited about my decision until football season was about to start. I became a little depressed, realizing how much I missed the game and that I'd never play it again in an organized situation.

I decided right before practice was about to start that I *had* to play football. I contacted both schools who'd showed interest in me earlier to see if they were still interested. The one that had offered the scholarship declined, but the other school was still interested, so I enrolled there.

Bobby Jones during his playing days as wide receiver for the New York Jets.

Photo by Warren Tribune Chronicle

Q: Would you do anything different if you had the chance to do it again?

A: I believed, as all young people do, that I had all the answers. *Wrong!* I should have looked to my parents and coaches more for advice. I should have talked with others who'd made similar decisions for their advice. The more input and knowledge one can gain from experience is a plus.

If given the opportunity to do it over, there are two possible changes I'd make. As I sit today, I'm not sure which direction I'd choose now that I've seen how my life developed.

One possibility is that when I made my choice to play football in college, I should have stayed there, given my best effort, and completed my education. The other possibility is that I believed very strongly in my ability to play on a Division I level. That opportunity never presented itself to me. If I had to do it over, I might walk on at a major university.

Q: What advice do you have for student athletes?

A: My advice to any young people is to believe in themselves. I encourage them to have dreams and goals. They need to understand that others whom they see as being successful in sports are no different than they are. The difference is the desire and willingness to pay the price to achieve one's dream. *It's better to have tried and failed than never to have tried at all!*

Q: What advice do you have for parents?

A: Support your child 100 percent in his/her desires; also make sure the student athlete is doing his/her very best in academics.

Q: Do you feel you need a break or a certain amount of luck to make it in professional sports?

A: Yes. I believe there's a certain amount of luck needed to accomplish anything. But I also believe that people make their own breaks and create their own luck. I'm a firm believer in *preparation and opportunity.* My meaning is that an individual never knows when an opportunity may knock, but when it does, you'd better be prepared to take advantage of that opportunity.

For example, I worked out every day for one whole year, not really knowing if I would actually get a tryout with the New York Jets. It looked for a while that it may not happen. It took another last try from Bill Kushner, a friend of mine, to finally convince the Jets to take a look at me. They finally agreed; the opportunity came; and I was prepared. I was at my best because of all the hard work I'd done.

Would that alone mean that I would make it? No! But I had done all the preparation, and I was ready. If I didn't get signed or make the team, at least I would have known that I'd done my best and that my ability wasn't good enough, but I would know that there would be no wondering. As I mentioned before: *There is no shame in failing— the shame is in never trying.*

Another example: Marcus Marek, an Ohio State freshman, was a backup linebacker for his first game or two. Then the starting linebacker in front of him got hurt; Marcus replaced him and never looked back. He was All-Big Ten and All-American, and he broke tackling records and other records. Recently, he was inducted into the OSU Hall of Fame.

The lesson to be learned? He prepared himself, and when his opportunity came in his freshman year, he was prepared to succeed. Was that luck? Maybe, but I tend to believe he earned it.

Q: Were any other athletes you played with or against in the NFL overlooked or not heavily recruited in high school?

A: Numerous other NFL players also weren't associated with major colleges or even Division I programs.

- Andre Reed, Kutztown U, Buffalo Bills wide receiver; will be a future Hall of Famer;

- Bruce Harper, Kutztown U, New York Jets; one of the all-time kick returners in the NFL;

- Mark Gastineau, Central Oklahoma, New York Jets defensive end; former NFL record holder for sacks in one season;

- Judson Flint, Farrell PA, Indiana U. of Pennsylvania; Atlanta Falcons and Cleveland Browns; and

- Jim Haslett, Indiana U. of Pennsylvania, current New Orleans Saints' head coach

When Andre Reed was a wide receiver in the Buffalo Bills' training camp, he came to me for advice on how to run pass routes. I taught Andre to run pass routes so well that I ended up retiring shortly after because the young Andre took my playing time away from me. Many other NFL players also weren't associated with major colleges or even Division I programs.

Q: What do you suggest that student athletes do to get noticed and promote themselves?

A: First of all, let your high-school coach know you want to play collegiate sports; then figure out what division level is best suited for your talents by asking your coach, attending sports camps, and comparing yourself to the talent around you. Ask the college coaches at camp what level they think you can play.

Be realistic about what talent level you're capable of playing at, and then send video tapes to those colleges in that level. Also send a professional and honest profile of yourself and your achievements, any newspaper clippings about yourself, and especially those in which an opposing coach speaks about you. Get credible former athletes, coaches, or alumni to write letters of recommendations for you.

Get good grades! Many times, a decision between two athletes competing for a scholarship comes down to which one of them has the better grades. The amount of money awarded may be affected by academic records.

Q: Do you think you have to come from a big high school to get an athletic scholarship?

A: No, I think a good program is more important. Brookfield High School is a good example. It had a graduating class of 100, and because of its program, several athletes went on to play at colleges and universities and the pros: Marcus Marek, Ohio State; Ed Pryts, Penn State; Darwin Ulmer, Arizona; John Lott, Michigan; Ken Bencetic, Kent State; Kenny Christello, Miami of Ohio; Bernie Carpenter, Clarion; Tom Volarich, Malone College; Chuck Barrington, Ohio University; Jay Leipheimer, Clarion; and Bob Trudo, Detroit Tigers. Other local high schools turned out good athletes, too: Ralph Stringer, North Carolina State and Atlanta Falcons; Randy Holloway, Pitt University, Minnesota Vikings; and Mike O'Connell, Cincinnati, NFL.

Q: **What's your opinion on sports camps?**

A: I would recommend a student athlete attend them, at least one, especially if he/she's looking for an opportunity to play sports beyond high school. I believe there are two reasons that attending a college camp can be useful for the student athlete:

1. for the instruction and information they would receive from knowledgeable coaches, and learning the correct drills and proper techniques would definitely help the athlete improve, and

2. to have the opportunity to evaluate him/herself honestly to see how his/her ability compares to other athletes. This will help determine which level of competition he/she could handle in college.

Q: **Do you think that there is an exact step-by-step process that a high-school athlete can follow that will guarantee an athletic scholarship?**

A: No. If you haven't realized that on your own, then continue reading to find out why there isn't one.

Author's note: *To you young people reading this inteview, here's the scoop on Bobby's size at different times in his early career: Jones was 5'3" and 110 lbs. in 9th grade. When he graduated from high school, he was 5'10" and 165 lbs.; four years later when he tried out for the New York Jets, he was 5'11" and 185 lbs.*

The Ken Tirpack Story, All-American, Twins Draft Choice, Indians' Scout

Ken's background includes attending Ohio State University on a partial scholarship. He went on to become a three-time All Big Ten Conference first-baseman and a 3rd-team All-American. He was then selected by the Minnesota Twins in the 20th round of the baseball draft. Ken played for six years in the minor leagues, two of those at the AA level. Currently, he's in his third year as a scout for the Cleveland Indians organization.

When Ken attended Campbell High School in Ohio, he received scholarship offers from various colleges in his region and only a partial scholarship offer from Ohio State. He believed in himself and his abilities and wanted to play baseball at the best level possible—*Big Ten*—and decided to play for Ohio State, even though they didn't offer him a full scholarship.

Needless to say, many people in his area thought that Ken was out of his mind for passing up the big money scholarships and said that he wouldn't ever be able to play at that level. But that didn't stop him, and did he ever prove them wrong! His outstanding performance on the field led to his receiving an athletic scholarship and a college education with a degree in business.

All of the negative comments from those who didn't believe in his abilities spurred Ken on. What they didn't know were the size of his heart and the amount of determination that motivated him daily. His size, considered small for a first-baseman—6' and 160 lbs. in high school and 180 lbs. at age 22 when he was drafted—didn't hold him back. Ken is a super example of getting what you want if you want it badly enough. Now he's a scout for the Cleveland Indians.

Q: What's your advice for high-school student athletes on getting what you want?

A: *Don't give up on your dreams!* Hustle on and off the field, work at your game, conduct yourself in a professional manner on the field, and most important: *Don't ever let somebody tell you that you aren't good enough when you know you are!*

Q: How does a baseball prospect go about getting noticed by professional scouts?

A: Play in the best leagues and tournaments possible. Play at the highest level of competition not only to get noticed but also to improve your game. Attend tryouts, showcases, and camps.

Author's note: *Ken was small for a first baseman at every level he played in, but he still produced at every level as he climbed the ladder from high school to college to the minor leagues. But his size finally caught up when he reached the top of the ladder—another real-life example of how hard it is to make it to the majors despite playing super ball at all lower levels.*

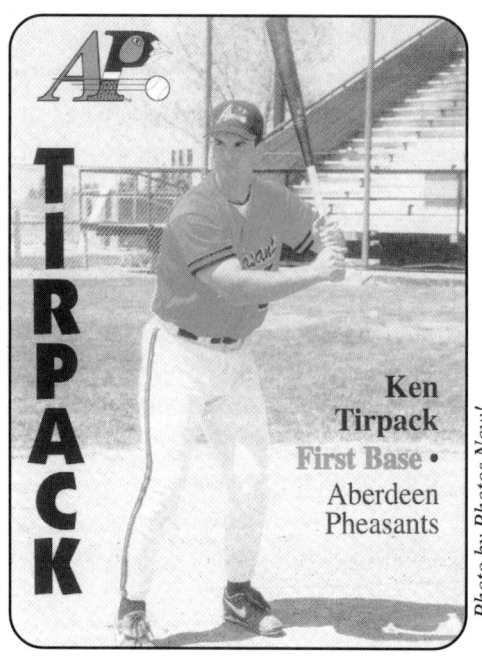

Ken Tirpack
First Base •
Aberdeen Pheasants

Photo by Photos Now!

The Mike Barnett Story, Major League Hitting Coach, Toronto Blue Jays

Not every inspirational story has to lead to the athlete becoming a professional athlete or an All-American, and the following story is an excellent example.

Mike's story is written for the young athletes who may have dreams of becoming a coach once their playing days are over.

Mike's background includes being a good high-school catcher for his Bexley High baseball team in Columbus, Ohio. Mike made the Ohio University baseball team as a walk-on. His college coaching experience includes being an assistant coach at both Ohio University and the University of Tennessee. He worked in the New York Yankees' organization for five years as Assistant Administrator of Baseball Operations and Video Director. He has coached professionally for the Chicago White Sox for eight years and the Arizona Diamondbacks for two years before becoming the hitting coach for the Toronto Blue Jays in 2002. He was the personal hitting coach for Michael Jordan while he was in the Chicago White Sox's organization.

Although Mike didn't receive much playing time at Ohio University during his college career because of a shoulder injury and the quality-level of competition that was ahead of him at a good Division I baseball program. This program included several great athletes who went on to become All-Americans, one of which was Bob Brenly, a former catcher for the San Francisco Giants and the current manager of the Arizona Diamondbacks. It didn't stop him from getting his degree in sports administration and learning all of the aspects of the game while becoming the ultimate team player, a teammate whom everybody on the team liked and respected and who would do whatever he could to help out the team.

When Mike's collegiate playing career was over, his coaching career began, and he became a graduate assistant coach for the Ohio University baseball team. With Ohio University being in Athens, less than an hour from Columbus, Mike was also able to become the bullpen catcher for the Columbus Clippers' minor league baseball team during its season. The Clippers played in the International League and were the AAA affiliate for the New York Yankees.

Because of Mike's upbeat personality, he was a positive team member who could and always would contribute to team morale; he had the ability to fit into any program. And needless to say, once the players, coaches, and front office from the New York Yankees got to know Mike, he was on his way to the Big Apple. As Assistant Administrator for Baseball Operations and Video Director, Mike assisted the major league coaches who analyzed films and tendencies of the Yankees' players.

This was a very exciting time for Mike, who was still in his 20's. The Yankees were well ahead of the other professional organizations at that point in the 1980's as far as using the art of technology. Mike initially helped analyze the art of pitching with pitching coach Clyde King and Dave Righetti, a Yankees' pitcher who is now with the San Francisco Giants. But with Mike's passionate desire to learn all aspects of the game, he would also stay and watch the breakdown of hitting films with Lou Pinella, Yankee's outfielder and current manager of the Seattle Mariners. Little did Mike know at that point n his career that he would eventually become a major league hitting coach. With his background during his playing days as a catcher, he figured he would become a pitching coach, especially since that was the reason for his going to the Big Apple in the first place.

Mike gives this advice to all of the young athletes who have dreams and goals of playing sports at the next level, whether it is in college or the pros:

"First of all, concentrate on getting a college education just so you have something to fall back on when your playing days are over. Anything can happen, and it doesn't always have to do with whether you're good enough or not. Your career may come to an end sooner that you expected for reasons such as an injury or a personal family matter that causes you to have to concentrate on making a living rather than playing baseball part-time. You're not going to make ends meet if you're playing only four to six months out of a year professionally in the minor leagues and you have personal responsibilities that need to be addressed. I tell all of the players on our Blue Jays' team who haven't completed their requirements for that college degree to make sure they take the necessary steps to get it, even if it's only a course or two per year during the off-season."

Barnett gives hitting tips prior to a Blue Jays' game against the Indians at Jacobs Field, in Cleveland, Ohio.

Q: What advice do you have for the high-school athlete who has the chance to sign a professional contract and go directly to playing professional baseball rather than playing collegiate baseball?

A: I personally suggest that the student athlete attend college or even a junior college to mature physically, to work on his/her game, and to begin working toward that college education. *My degree in sports administration certainly helped me get my foot in the door with the New York Yankees' organization.* Many young athletes have a visual image of professional baseball being played in major league stadiums where thousands of fans watch them play in person or on TV. This is not the case; the high-school athlete will not be going directly to a major league team, but instead will be playing minor league baseball for several years. More than likely, they will be doing all of their traveling to away games by bus. They also will be playing on teams with players who are older and more mature than they are— both mentally and physically. Our Toronto organization is now leaning towards drafting or signing prospects out of college rather than high school for this very reason.

Q: As a former college coach, what advice do you have for the parents concerning the recruiting process that leads to athletic scholarships?

A: You get only one chance for an athletic scholarship. Learn as much about the recruiting process as you can before it's too late to do anything about it. The longer you take to understand the process, the less likely your chances of every getting an athletic scholarship.

When I asked Mike's college coach Jerry France if he was surprised that Mike was now the major league hitting coach for the Toronto Blue Jays, Coach France said, "No, not at all. Everybody liked Mike. How could you not like him? Mike had the most unbelievable attitude of any player I've every coached. Here's a kid who batted one time in his entire collegiate baseball career, and you would have thought he was a starter who was having a great season because of the way he acted each and every day. Mike's personality and ability to communicate are just as much the reasons for his now being Toronto's hitting coach as is the amount of knowledge he has acquired for the art of teaching hitting."

Q: What advice do you have for young athletes who may want to become a coach after their playing days are over?

A: Learn as much as you can about the fundamentals of the position that you will be coaching, and learn as much about the mindset of the competition your player will be facing.

Example one: If you're coaching a hitter, you need to tell the player you're coaching that he/she needs to have an understanding of pitching also. You need to help out your player mentally so that he/she knows the objective of the pitcher who is trying to get him/her out. The pitcher is being taught by his/her pitching coach to move the ball abound the plate and to pitch low and outside and then high and inside.

Example two: If you're teaching and coaching a wide receiver in football, you need to help him learn and understand what the defender is being taught by his defensive backs' coach in order to keep your athlete from being successful.

The more information you can provide (teach) athletes to help them understand the objective of the competition they will face, the more success you and your athlete will have.

Q: Do you have any quick tips on hitting for young baseball players?

A: The key to hitting is *having the proper mindset*. The hitter's mindset, whether it is in practice or in the game, should be to think about driving the ball (hitting line drives.)

The hitter needs to imagine that the pitcher will be throwing to his weaknesses (a pitch low and on the outside half of the plate), and he/she needs to gear his/her swing to hit (drive) that pitch to the opposite field. If the pitch happens to be inside, then all the hitter needs to do is react to the inside pitch by turning on the ball (turning his hips).

All you young hitters need to know is that if a college coach or a professional scout watches you take batting practice, he will be more impressed with you, your swing, and hitting potential if you can hit line drives to the opposite field when the pitch is outside rather than trying to pull that pitch in for a home run. That pitch that you can pull for a home run in batting practice is coming in much slower than it will be during an actual game situation.

Young hitters need to learn how to hit the ball where it is pitched and to use all parts of the field to their advantage. The keys to hitting, once again, are having the proper mindset and being disciplined enough to use that mindset at all times—not just during a game but even more, when you practice. Keep in mind that a professional scout or college recruiter is going to come to your ball game well ahead of time to watch you take batting and infield practice to check out your work habits.

Author's note: *What Mike, a former teammate of mine at Ohio University has accomplished while batting only one time in his college baseball career should be very inspirational to all you young athletes who hope to become a coach someday when your playing days are over. When his playing career came to an end because of a shoulder injury, he had the insight to know well ahead of time how important his college education would be to him in his future. His education opened the door to his first opportunity in Major League baseball and as they say the rest is history.*

The Zack Walz Story, Arizona Cardinals' Linebacker, Dartmouth College All-American

Zack Walz's story is a great example of how a talented high-school athlete can go unnoticed during the athletic recruiting process. Zack refused to give up on his dreams of playing football at the college level when he was not offered an athletic scholarship during his senior year at St. Francis High School in Mountain View, California. Because of his persistent nature, he knew his future included playing college football. He decided to take matters into his own hands and promote himself to colleges all across the country. Countless hours of compiling videotape, cutting highlight films and answering questionnaires finally paid off. With his excellent high school grades, several Ivy League schools showed interest and offered Zack campus visits. He chose Dartmouth College, a Division I-AA school in Hanover, New Hampshire, where he went on to become only the third player in Ivy League history to earn first-team All-Ivy honors three straight years. He also received All-American honors and became the third leading tackler in Dartmouth history. His storied football career continued when he was selected by the Arizona Cardinals in the 6th-round of the 1998 NFL draft. Undersized and underestimated, he surprised more naysayers as he became a standout special-teams's player and won the starting outside linebacker position for two of this four years there.

Q: How valuable to you was having good grades in high school?

A: The way I look at it, my hard work in the classroom paved the way for me to have a tremendous football career. Indeed, I was blessed with athletic prowess and playing football just came easy. Like so many other kids though, I go lost in the frenzied nightmare that is college recruiting. My grades ultimately separated me form a swarm of college football hopefuls and helped me to graduate form Dartmouth College and enjoy an amazing NFL career.

Q: In your high-school senior year, the national letter of intent signing period has passed, and you realized that you weren't going to get an athletic scholarship without promoting yourself

to college coaches. What did you do to keep motivated and stay focused on pursuing your dreams when it seemed that you might not be able to play football at the next level?

A: I truly believed in myself and in my abilities to play football. I felt that if I continued to saturate the coaching world with my game films and highlights, someone eventually, would take notice. I kept after it through scores of rejections and finally put together a recruiting package that caught some interest.

Q: What do you suggest that student athletes do be noticed and recruited.

A: As a high-school athlete, I was caught up by the notion that "good" football existed only on the major college level. My dreams were to play in the NFL, and I thought the only way to get there would be through a top Division I college. My advice to high-school students across the country is to take what you can get. Don't force yourself into a program where you might get lost in the shuffle and may never play. Send your game films and highlights to schools in every division all across the country. These days smaller colleges send just as many players to the next level as major colleges. If your dreams are to play in the NFL and you're good enough, they'll find you no matter where you go to school. And you'll probably wind up having a better college experience altogether.

Authors note: *Zack is a great example of an athlete "giving something back to the game." As an overlooked high-school player, he founded a company called DVD Recruiting to help athletes just like himself effectively promote themselves to college coaches. They create Personalized Video Discs (PVD's) for distribution to college coaches. To findout more about DVD Recruiting, go to page 182 in the Recruiting Services chapter or visit www.dvdrecruiting.com*

Zack, at 27 years old, puts his college education to good use after his career ending football injury, as the president of DVD Recruiting located in Tempe, Arizona.

ADVICE

FROM

"THE PROS"

Advice from Paul Maguire, NFL Analyst for ESPN

Currently, Paul is an ESPN football analyst on Sunday night's NFL broadcast team with Mike Patrick and Joe Theisman. Maguire began his football career at Ursuline High School, Youngstown, Ohio. He accepted an athletic scholarship for football at The Citadel, playing end for four years; as a senior, he led the nation with 11 touchdowns. Paul was selected as All-Southern Conference and inducted into the South Carolina Hall of Fame.

His 11-year AFL career began as a linebacker with the Los Angeles Chargers who later moved to San Diego; there his record-setting punt of 86 yards still stands today. He continued his career with the Buffalo Bills, where he established virtually all of Buffalo's punting records.

Maguire moved from the playing field into the broadcasting field, where he has been an NBC analyst for AFC telecasts and then host of the all-day live NFL draft for ESPN. He's consistently received national attention in many highly regarded publications: *Sports Illustrated,* the *New York Times, Los Angeles Times, USA Today,* and *TV Guide.* In *People Magazine*'s News and Views, Larry King asks: "Have you noticed that Paul Maguire has become on of the best color analysts in broadcasting today?"

Paul returns every year to his hometown to "give something back to the game" at the Ursuline Alumni annual scholarship dinner, established by Paul to honor his high-school coach, Nick Johnson. Johnson helped Maguire get his scholarship to The Citadel. Proceeds go to the Nick Johnson Scholarship Fund to benefit athletes from Ursuline, a private Catholic school.

Q: What advice can you add to this scholarship guide to help get the message across to student athletes that they need "Plan B" to fall back on (a college education)?

(Paul's answer was short and to the point!)

A: Today's young athletes need to know that their "Plan A" must be getting a college education—NOT their "Plan B." The chances of getting an athletic scholarship are very slim, and the chances of ever becoming a professional athlete are even many times more difficult.

Q: **What do parents have to know about athletic scholarships?**

A: They have to research the actual percentages of how many high-school athletes actually receive athletic scholarships, let alone progress to the professional level. The approximate number of high-school students who get athletic scholarships are one out of a hundred—.01 percent. Be realistic while you're striving to help your athlete. Stress the percentages so that they, too, can be realistic about the difficulty of obtaining their dreams and goals.

Q: **What should be the main goal of student athletes who want to be involved in collegiate sports?**

A: Your dreams and goals should be making sure that you acquire a college education first and foremost! Your "Plan B" should be playing sports at the next level, whether it's collegiately or professionally.

Q: **Do you feel that there is an exact step-by-step process that a high-school athlete can follow that guarantees an athletic scholarship?**

A: No, there are only a limited number of athletic scholarships available to begin with, and basically, it comes down to two things: 1. talent—either you are good enough to play at the next level or you're not, in the eyes of the college recruiters, and 2. grades—the better your grades are, the better your chances of being recruited athletically. All you young athletes need to keep in mind that if you have good grades and don't get an athletic scholarship, those good grades are sure going to come in real handy when it comes time to apply for financial aid and academic scholarships to pay for college.

Photo by Bob Knuff

Paul receives a gift of appreciation from Jason McCrae at the Ursuline High School Alumni annual Nick Johnson Scholarship Dinner in Youngstown, Ohio, as the main speaker, CBS Sports analyst Solomon Wilcots (sitting), looks on. Jason was one of the first Ursuline High School student athletes to receive a Nick Johnson scholarship 14 years ago.

Author's note: *Paul is an excellent example of an athlete "giving something back to the game," through his numerous resources and connections in the sports arena. He has been able to have some of the most recognizable sports figures ever as main speakers at the Nick Johnson Scholarship Dinner. Bob Costas, Paul Hornung, Bart Starr, Chris Berman, Len Dawson, Rocky Blier, Ron Jaworski, Phil Simms, Steve Tasker, Carmen Policy, Ozzie Newsome, Dante Lavelli, Solomon Wilcots, and Ed O'Neill (a former Ursuline High School graduate) have all been the main speakers at this fund-raising scholarship dinner.*

Advice from Solomon Wilcots, CBS Broadcaster

Photo by Bob Knuff

Solomon is currently a game analyst on *The NFL on CBS* and is on *March Madness*, the NCAA's college basketball tournament. He is also a sports anchor at an NBC affiliate in Cincinnati, Ohio, where he does feature reports on local high-school teams. Previously, he was a studio anchor for Fox Sports Net college football and then an ESPN reporter for NFL games.

In high school, Solomon played defensive back in Compton, California. He and nine others received Division I scholarships. At the University of Colorado, he was a starting cornerback for two years and earned All-Big Eight honors in his senior year. He was team captain and majored in English literature.

The Cincinnati Bengals drafted him in the 8th round as a cornerback, where he played for four seasons before moving on to the Vikings for a year and then to the Steelers for another year.

At the close of his playing career, Wilcots became a broadcasting intern in Cincinnati, where he now resides. He learned all facets of broadcasting: reporting, feature writing, column writing, editing, and producing—except photography.

Q: What advice do you have for student athletes who want to get an athletic scholarship?

A: First of all, remember how difficult it is to get an athletic scholarship. Only one percent of high-school senior athletes actually receive them.

Understand the importance of earning good grades and how they affect your chances of even being considered as a potential recruit by college coaches. Good grades show your coaches a good work ethic, and it increases your chances of getting an athletic scholarship and financial assistance—very important if you participate in a sport that offers only partial scholarships or plan to go into a division level that doesn't actually offer athletic scholarships.

Be realistic in assessing your athletic abilities when you start to make choices about colleges to visit or to attend. Are you talented enough to play at the division level that you have your sights on? Are they recruiting at your position? Are there already many talented underclassmen waiting in line to become the starter for that position? Are there others in your recruiting class who've already been recruited?

I grew up in Compton, not far from the UCLA campus in Los Angeles. I always rooted for the Bruins and would have loved to play for them. I visited the campus and was offered a scholarship, but I researched the roster and discovered that their program was so heavily stocked with talented underclassmen who played my position that even in the best case scenario, I didn't feel that I would ever see much playing time for several years to come.

I visited two other colleges to see which was best suited for my athletic and academic abilities. Then since I had time for one more visit before the signing deadline, I checked out the University of Colorado because I still hadn't decided. There, I found what I was looking for. It was a feeling that I didn't experience at the other colleges even though they had great athletic and academic programs.

Q: What advice do you have for the student athlete who is fortunate enough to get an athletic scholarship?

A: Decide what you're going to do with it! Will you use the investment that the college made in you by paying for your education to progress and become a productive member of society, or will you go to school just to play a sport?

Q: What advice do you have for parents who want to see their children attend college on an athletic scholarship?

A: First of all, be realistic with yourself as a parent—are you more excited about your child attending on a scholarship than he/she is?

Second, while supporting and discussing your child's dreams of playing sports in college, are you making sure that both parties are being realistic about his/her talent level? Is your child a very good high-school athlete or dominating in his/her sport? Usually the athletes who dominate get the scholarships. Not getting a scholarship doesn't mean that he/she isn't a good athlete—it simply means that he/she didn't dominate. Remember that the primary reason to attend college is to get an education, regardless of sports participation.

Q: What advice do you have about using supplements?

A: *Stay away from them!* Just because they're legal and sold over the counter doesn't mean they're good for you. Once in your system, they can act like a steroid and begin to build your testosterone level. You don't want this to happen to your body because too many problems arise, like dehydration that causes organs to start to shut down and in some cases can be fatal.

Build strength and gain weight to improve your chances of becoming a better athlete simply through a good nutritional diet. There's no reason to jeopardize your health just to become better in your sport.

Q: Why did you retire after playing only six years in the NFL when you could have played longer?

A: I wanted to walk away from the game I loved, literally walk away, as a healthy individual to spend time with my wife and watch my children grow up. I had my college education to fall back on, and I used that to learn the broadcasting business.

Q: Any other advice for student athletes as far as their dreams and goals of becoming a collegiate or professional athlete?

A: *Be realistic!* It's very difficult to make it to the next level; collegiate and professional sports can be very physically demanding of both your time and your body, and you have to ask yourself what you're going to do when your playing days are over.

And get your college education! Make that your priority. Research the colleges that offer the courses and majors you are interested in. Play your sport with pride and respect, display good sportsmanship, and remember that opposing coaches pick you for the All-Conference, All-County, All-State teams, Player of the Year awards, etc. High-school coaches are very often asked by colleges coaches who the better players are that they know of, and when opposing players are sent questionnaires, they are asked about the best players they know or have played against. You could miss out on many opportunities to have your name heard by college coaches and, therefore, being noticed because of your actions on or off the field.

And I suggest that all young athletes read, *When Pride Still Mattered, A Life of Vince Lombardi*

Q: Do you feel that there is an exact step-by-step process that a high-school athlete can follow to guarantee an athletic scholarship?

A: No, there are too many factors, incidentals, variables, and so few scholarships available for the number of athletes needing one.

Solomon speaks to the audience at the Ursuline High School Alumni annual Nick Johnson Scholarship Dinner in Youngstown, Ohio. Solomon was chosen as the main speaker and special guest by his close friend, ESPN football anaylst Paul Maguire, sitting in the background. Maguire establsed the scholarship dinner to honor his high-school coach Nick Johnson and to benefit student athletes from his alma mater with scholarships.

Advice from Michael Zordich, Penn State All-American and NFL Player

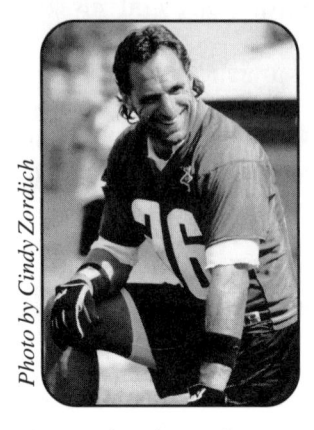

Photo by Cindy Zordich

Michael was an All-Ohio High School football player for Youngstown Chaney High School; an All-American defensive back for Joe Paterno at Penn State; a 12-year NFL veteran, playing defensive back for the New York Jets, Arizona Cardinals, and Philadelphia Eagles; and twice selected to the All-Madden Team. Formerly the defensive backfield coach for the Youngstown (Ohio) Cardinal Mooney High School football team, he's currently a vice president at Wright Industries, Pittsburgh, Pennsylvania, underground utilities contractors, and a youth league football coach.

Q: What do college coaches look for when recruiting student athletes, other than their physical tools?

A: A well-rounded person—somebody who is good at home, good in school, and involved somehow in the community. They're looking for people with character, people who aren't afraid to work, who have discipline and can work well with others.

Q: Do you have any advice for high-school student athletes on the collegiate athletic recruiting experience?

A: Take advantage of the experience; see as many campuses as you can. Ask as many questions as you can. The more you know helps make your decision easier.

Q: Do you have any advice for the parents on the recruiting process?

A: Same as the last question, but in the end, I believe that students should make the choice with some guidance from their parents, only if the parents are involved in the *whole* process.

Q: Do you have any advice for junior high athletes who dream of playing sports in college or the NFL?

A: Take one step at a time; it's very difficult to keep progressing to the next level. Keep your mind focused to what's at hand; be the best at what you do now.

Q: What are the most difficult factors involved in the transition from the high-school sports level to the collegiate sports level?

A: Everything you do is different because you're on your own. You must be strong-minded; school is much harder; sports are much harder because of the increased competition. It's important to have fun in college, but you must know how to handle [and balance] your academic workload with your sports workload.

Q: How important do you feel that it was for you to have gotten your college education and how has it helped you?

A: Extremely important! Even though I didn't go into the field that I had studied for in college, I developed transferrable skills. I feel that the time required of me for classwork, library research, and the athletic classroom/practice field/meeting room setting led me to acquire the disciplinary skills needed to successfully manage my time.

Basically, the biggest asset I gained from college was understanding the meaning of self-discipline and how necessary it was for me to manage two different career objectives at the same time in college. I had to learn how to balance my time by getting my academic work straight while giving all I could athletically to my sport. Learning this at a young age gave me skills I could use in the future.

Definitely, my college education was good to me; it was fun, and I met a lot of good people. And now that my NFL football career is over, the discipline and time-management skills I learned in college are directly coming into play even though I'm in a different field than that which I studied.

Zordich returns an interception for the Philadelphia Eagles.

Photo by Cindy Zordich

80

Michael Zordich during his playing days for the Arizona Cardinals.

Author's note: *Michael Zordich was originally drafted by the San Diego Chargers in the 9th round and released later that year during training camp. Michael "never gave up on his dreams" of being an NFL football player and tried out for the New York Jets the next season. He went on to have a successful 12-year NFL career.*

Michael's wife Cynthia is the author of When the Clock Runs Out, *a fascinating book that tells the true stories of what many former athletes have encountered in life after their playing days are over. You can find this book at your local bookstore, and you can check out her website, www.behindthecage.com, to find out more about the book, as well as being able to view many real-life photos of professional athletes taken by Cynthia on the sidelines of NFL games. "Behind the cage" was Michael's saying when he put his helmet on. When it was time for serious football, he'd say to his teammates, "Let's go! It's time to get behind the cage!"*

I sincerely recommend this book to all student athletes, coaches, and parents so that they can get a real-life perspective on the realities of sports during and after an athlete's career.

Advice from Scott Knox, Pittsburgh Pirates' Free Agent, Former College Coach

Scott's background includes playing collegiate baseball at Manatee Community Junior College in Florida, transferring to Kentucky University where he was signed as a free agent by the Pittsburgh Pirates' organization, and playing professionally for three years. He was an All-State athlete in four sports while playing at Columbiana High School in Ohio. His coaching experience includes serving as the head baseball coach at Youngstown State University and currently as head coach at Boardman High School, Youngstown, Ohio. Scott is also president of the Line-Drive Baseball Academy. Even though Scott is a high-school baseball coach from Ohio, he has coached numerous athletes who have received Division I baseball scholarships all across the country, such as Georgia Tech, Notre Dame, University of South Carolina, and the University of Tennessee. Many of the other players he coached elected to go the junior-college route because of Scott's background and connections in that area; Manatee Community College in Florida, Garrett Community in Maryland, and Joliet Junior College in Illinois.

Q: **Do you have any advice for high-school student athletes on the athletic recruiting process?**

A: The most important thing to remember is that the athlete is a student *first*. GPA and ACT/SAT scores will determine where the athlete needs to narrow his/her choices after qualifying academically. Then his/her athletic skills will determine at what level he/she may compete. The athletes' junior year is the key year.

Q: **Do you have any advice for the parents on the athletic recruiting process?**

A: Don't wait for anyone to do the work for you; money doesn't fall from the sky. Players need to market themselves starting in their sophomore year in high school—camps, recruiting services, showcases, etc.

Q: Do you have any advice for junior-high student athletes who want to get an athletic scholarship in the future?

A: The junior-high student athlete needs to have great study habits. He/she must know that the GPA starts in the freshman year.

Q: What's your opinion on sports camps? Should student athletes attend camps?

A: Any time athletes can expose themselves to coaches and scouts, it can only help them.

Q: Can you explain how attending a junior college can be beneficial to student athletes? And are junior colleges just for student athletes who don't have good enough grades to be accepted at NCAA colleges?

A: Junior colleges are two-year schools. The academic hours transfer over to four-year institutions. The first two years are basic classes wherever you go before anyone gets into his/her major. The junior college avenue allows flexibility when transferring to a four-year school It also may allow athletes to compete earlier in their freshman year.

Q: What do you suggest is the best way for student athletes to find out what division level is best-suited for their athletic and academic abilities?

A: The high-school coach helps, along with getting feedback from potential college coaches. Camps, showcases, and recruiting services also will aid in their decision.

Q: Do you feel that student athletes' chances of being recruited increase if college coaches know that they will be receiving academic money for college because of good grad*es?*

A: Every college coach loves to deal with an athlete who he/she knows will be eligible for the team.

Q: What do you suggest that student athletes do to be noticed and recruited?

A: Camps, showcases, and recruiting services. *Student athletes must market themselves!*

Q: Describe your recruiting and collegiate sports experience as a ball player

A: I attended Manatee Junior College in Florida my first year in college. It had nothing to do with grades. I wanted to play baseball in Florida. That was the avenue the four-year colleges in the South suggested I go. I then transferred to the University of Kentucky for two years before signing with the Pittsburgh Pirates. Later at Class A Prince William, Carolina League, in the minors, I played center field along with Barry Bonds in left field and Bobby Bonilla in right field.

Q: Would you do anything different if you had the chance to do it again?

A: I would do *exactly* the same thing. The junior college route marketed my talents to the four-year schools.

Q: How important do you feel it was for you to have earned your college education? How has it helped you?

A: Getting my college education was essential. I wouldn't have been able to become a teacher without it. For you youngsters out there: Earning a college education is the only thing! You should be thinking that it's essential unless you want to work for minimum wage the rest of your life.

Scott puts his college education (B.S. in Ed.) to good use as a high-school gym teacher.

Advice from Jeff Faine, Cleveland Browns' 1st-round Draft Pick, Notre Dame All-American

Jeff's background includes receiving a football scholarship to the University of Notre Dame. He played his high-school football at Seminole High School in Sanford, Florida. Jeff was selected to the *USA Today's* All-American Team while in high school and to the ESPN.com and *The Sporting News* All-American Teams while in college. He was chosen in the 1st–round of the NFL draft by the Cleveland Browns with the 21st pick overall. He received his college degree in communications in four years.

Q: What advice do you have for the junior-high and high-school student athletes who have dreams and goals of receiving an athletic scholarship?

A: Many youngsters overlook the importance of having good grades. They need to know that the recruiting process that leads to athletic scholarships begins with grades and that athleticism is secondary. What good is athleticism if you're not eligible to step onto the playing field? Like the old adage goes, everything starts with smarts.

Q: How important do you feel your college education will be to you once your playing days are over?

A: Having my college education will be tremendously important to me once my playing days are over. Even though I have already graduated from college and have my degree, I'm still not finished learning. I am going to go back to college to take more courses in finances in the spring after my first season with the Browns even though I currently have a financial advisor to help me with my finances. I want to take more classes in business and finances so I can better understand everything my advisor is telling me that I should do with my money.

Headed for the National Football League

Advice from Matt Wilhelm, All-American Linebacker, The Ohio State University 2002 National Champions

Matt's background includes being selected as an All-Ohio linebacker while at Elyria Catholic High School in Lorain, Ohio. Matt received a football scholarship to play for The Ohio State University, where he was an All-American middle linebacker on this year's 2002 national championship team. His major is communications.

This interview took place at an autograph signing in March 2003, two months after Ohio State's victory over the University of Miami, Florida, in the Fiesta Bowl in Tempe, Arizona, and approximately one month before the NFL draft in April.

Q: What advice do you have for high-school athletes who have dreams of obtaining an athletic scholarship?

A: Young kids need to know that athletic scholarships are not given to just good players on a high-school team with a 10-0 record. There is so much more involved in earning an athletic scholarship. Sure, it helps to have the added exposure that comes with playing on a really good high-school team, but there is so much more involved concerning the recruiting process and earning an athletic scholarship. Athletes need to have the proper mindset and know that they must work hard at improving their skills and strengths in their particular sport. They need to know that being a good athlete requires a 12-month-a-year commitment to becoming a better athlete.

Q: **What advice do you have for parents of high-school athletes who hope to earn an athletic scholarship?**

A: The parents and their children must form a team; together they must be able to communicate openly and honestly about the young student athlete's dreams and goals. Also, the parents must support their children's decisions and allow them to make their own decisions about what college they wish to attend and also whether they want to play sports in college or not.

Q: **Do you feel junior high and high-school athletes should attend sports camps?**

A: Yes, sports camps are a great place to get exposure and to get valuable advice and tips on playing your position(s) in your particular sport.

Q: **What are you doing now to improve your chances of becoming a high-round NFL draft pick?**

A: I am working every day at improving all aspects of my game. I was invited to attend the NFL scouting combine in Indianapolis, Indiana, in February. (At this combine prospective professional football players are tested for their skills in the 40-yard dash, vertical and broad jumps, position-specific agility drills, bench press, and the wonderlic test, which tests future employees' cognitive ability.) I also recently took part in the Pro Day that was held in Columbus, which is an opportunity for all Ohio State draft-eligible seniors to impress NFL scouts. I have very high aspirations, and I am confident that I have the talent to succeed at the next level. I felt like I gave the scouts some quality workouts at the camps, and I received positive feedback but at this point I won't even try to guess what might happen. As we get closer to the April draft, I expect I'll have a better feel for what might take place. All it takes is for one team to take a liking to you come draft day.

Q: **What part of your game do you feel you can improve on the most?**

A: Leverage—because I am 6'4" tall and weigh 240 lbs., I am constantly trying to improve my leverage to go along with my size. I need to be able to get lower than the person blocking me. Then I can get the necessary leverage needed to fight him off and stay involved in the play while trying to make the tackle on the ball carrier at the same time.

Q: When asked by a junior-high linebacker at this autograph signing if he had any tips for young linebackers, Matt said:

A: "The key to becoming a great linebacker, besides having the talent and the skills to play that position, is preparation. Anything you can do to learn more about what your opponent is trying to do is a 'must.' You need to watch films of your opponent to observe their tendencies. Being that you are a junior-high linebacker who doesn't have access to game films as do the professional, collegiate, and high-school athletes, you have your work cut out for you. You still must prepare yourself mentally for all that can happen during a game situation and observe your opponent's tendencies and react accordingly while you're playing in that game.

Author's note: *Matt was selected in the fourth round of the 2003 NFL draft by the San Diego Chargers.*

Matt signs an autograph at the Eastwood Mall in Niles, Ohio for nine-year-old Joey Tuchek (L). Standing are Ken Kollar, mall general manager, and Joe Tuchek with his daughter, Nikki.

Advice from Kelly Holcomb, Cleveland Browns' Quarterback

Kelly's background includes receiving a football scholarship to Middle Tennessee State University. He played his high-school football at Lincoln County High School in Fayetteville, Tennessee. Kelly was inducted into the Tennessee Scholastic Collegiate Hall of Fame in 1994. He is a seven-year NFL veteran who has played for the Indianapolis Colts and the Cleveland Browns despite never being drafted by the NFL out of college.

Q: What advice do you have for high-school student athletes who have dreams of playing collegiate and pro sports?

A: Young athletes need to know that it is up to them to make their dreams happen. It is up to them to believe in themselves even when others may not. Look at me; I have been playing in the NFL for seven years even though I went to a small college and was not even drafted by an NFL team. Even though there were many people who didn't believe in my abilities along the way, I had to continue to believe in myself and keep working hard at my game to reach my dream of playing in the NFL. There were rough times when things weren't looking so good for me, but I refused to let anybody destroy my confidence and keep me from believing in myself.

Q: How important do you feel your college education will be to you once your playing days are over?

A: Very important! I received my degree in exercise science, which not only gives me something to look forward to but also something to fall back on a when my playing days are over. Young athletes need to know that their "Plan A" must be getting their college education and that their "Plan B" is their dreams of playing collegiate or professional sports.

Advice from Professional Scouts

Senior professional scouts from pro baseball teams offer their advice about engaging in sports and getting college educations. The bottom line? *Be realistic!*

Ray Vince—senior scout for the Seattle Mariners

My advice to any youngsters who are interested in becoming major league baseball players is that you need to ask yourself, "Do I really love the game?" because there will be times when things aren't going to go so well for you and you're going to ask yourself, "Why am I still playing this game?" You may ask yourself this question when you are in high school, college, or the minor leagues. If your answer at any point during hard times when you may not be playing so well is anything other than "I love the game," then you shouldn't be attempting to make it to the major leagues in the first place.

My advice to the parents who think that their child will be a major league baseball player some day is to be realistic. You need to know that the chances of your son making it to the major leagues are basically the same as your chances of hitting the lottery. Make sure your child gets a college education at some time in his/her life.

Mike Trbovich, senior scout for the Colorado Rockies

My advice to the Little League, junior-high, and high-school baseball players is to play the game, play as many games as possible, play with as much passion for the game as possible, play at the highest level of competition as possible.

If you're bigger, stronger, and better than the competition at the level you're playing at now, then move up to the next level of competition even if you're a younger age than that level. The only way you'll get better is by playing against good competition.

My advice for the parents is to watch your child play the game, enjoy watching your child play the game, and let the coach do the coaching of the game.

Many children dream of making it to the big leagues, but the chances of making the big leagues decrease every year with the number of players being signed at younger ages from other countries outside of the United States. At this point in time, only two percent of the baseball players who ever sign a professional contract ever make it to the big leagues, and approximately 1.5 percent of those ball players are from the United States.

If you have a choice between going to college on a scholarship and signing a professional contract, you and your parents need to consider all of the factors involved in that decision. A college education is a very valuable asset to fall back on once your playing days are over.

Dick Coury, senior scout for the Pittsburgh Pirates

I can't begin to explain how difficult it is to make it to the major leagues—the chances are so remote for a young ball player to make it these days. There are more professional minor league teams with more professional players, which leads to fewer chances and more competition. You need to have exceptional skills and a genuine love for the game to even have a chance to make it to the major leagues.

The percentages of making it to the big leagues are so small that you seriously need to consider getting your college education so that you have something to fall back on.

ADVICE FROM THE "COACHES' CORNER"

Advice from Ron Stoops Jr., of the Famous Coaching Family

Ron Jr.'s background includes playing football and basketball at Cardinal Mooney High School, Youngstown, Ohio. He was the defensive coordinator of football at Boardman High School in Ohio, and coaches now at Cardinal Mooney High School. Ron has coached numerous athletes who have received Division I football scholarships to colleges all across the country, such as Miami of Florida, Penn State, Georgia Tech, Michigan, the University of Pittsburgh, West Virginia, and North Carolina State University. He comes from a very strong and well-known athletic background. His dad, the late Ron Sr., was a well-respected football and baseball coach for many years, and his three brothers are now college coaches.

Ron's family has received a deserving amount of national recognition recently because two of his brothers coached the 2000 National Champion Oklahoma Sooners: Bobby was head coach and selected college football's Coach of the Year and Mike was the associate head coach. Their other brother, Mark, coaches the University of Miami's Hurricanes, the 2001 National Champions.

Bob Stoops: University of Iowa—honorable mention, All-American defensive back, two-time All Big Ten; head coach of 2000 National Champion Oklahoma Sooners; assistant coach at the University of Florida, Kansas State, and the University of Iowa.

Mike Stoops: University of Iowa—All-American defensive back, two-time All Big Ten; associate head coach of 2000 National Champion Oklahoma Sooners, Kansas State, University of Iowa. Current head coach for the University of Arizona.

Mark Stoops: three-year letterman at University of Iowa; coach at University of Miami Florida, the 2001 National Champs; University of Houston; University of Wyoming; University of South Florida. Current defensive coordinator for the University of Arizona.

Photo by Paul Gregory

Left to right: Ron with his uncle Bob, defensive football coach for four Division I-AA Youngstown State University Division national championship teams; his brother Bobby, head football coach for the 2000 University of Oklahoma national championship team and 2000 college football "Coach of the Year," his brother Mike, associate head football coach and defensive coordinator for the University of Oklahoma 2000 national championship team; and his brother Mark, defensive backs coach for the University of Miami 2001 national championship team.

Q: With all the experience in your family from both the high-school and collegiate levels, can you explain to student athletes and their parents what college recruiters look for when they're recruiting student athletes?

A: They all start by asking if the recruit is a good person—character is most important to them. They also want to know if the student athlete has good work habits and is reliable; next they want to know if he's a competitor and plays hard all of the time or just gets by.

Q: What's your opinion on college sports camps? Should student athletes attend these camps?

A: Student athletes should be selective; they need to have a realistic chance to be recruited by that school to make it worthwhile. There should be some contact between the recruit and the coaches prior to attending that camp.

Q: Do you have any advice for high-school student athletes on the athletic recruiting process?

A: Be polite and enthusiastic about all of the schools and coaches. Many times, athletes turn off coaches from smaller schools because they're getting attention from bigger schools. When the larger schools back off, the student athlete has nowhere to turn. I've seen this happen too many times!

Q: **Do you have any advice for junior-high student athletes with aspirations of playing a collegiate sport?**

A: Make sure you concentrate on your academics; younger athletes sometimes don't realize the importance of this until it's too late. Your grades in 9th grade are just as important as your grades in 12th grade when it comes to your overall GPA. Off-season training is a *must*!

Q: **Do you have any advice for the parents on the athletic recruiting process?**

Ron, also a junior high basketball coach, gives shooting tips to his sons Johnny (L) and Joey (R).

A: Encourage your child to keep an open mind and to keep as many options open as possible. Find out as much as possible about each university in regard to academics and athletics. Ask questions about how your child will fit in. Questions about graduation rates, job placement, tutors, playing time, etc., are reasonable to ask.

Q: What are the most important factors that you believe student athletes should be aware of in the transition from the high-school to the collegiate sports level?

A: The competition in the classroom and on the playing field is certain to be more intense in college than in high school. In college, all of the members of the team were high-school stars. Be prepared to handle the freedom that goes with college. You must have *discipline*!

Q: Do you think there is an exact step-by-step process that a high-school athlete can follow that guarantees him/her an athletic scholarship?

A: No, there are just too many variables involved in the athletic recruiting process for there to be an exact step-by-step process to follow. Each and every recruiting situation is unique. The more you read in this book, the better understanding you'll have of just how many variables actually come into play during the recruiting process.

Ron Jr., with his sister, Kathy (L), and his mother, Dee Dee, at the Cardinal Mooney High School Athletic Hall of Fame Banquet and Ron Stoops Scholarship Dinner named in honor of the memory of Ron's father, a well-respected high-school football coach.

Advice from Thom McDaniels, *USA Today*'s High-school Coach of the Year

Thom was selected as the *USA Today's High School Coach of the Year* as a reward for his success as the head football coach of Ohio Canton McKinley's 1997 *USA Today's* National Championship High School Team of the Year. He has been coaching high-school football for 29 years and is currently the head football coach for Warren Harding High School in Warren, Ohio. *Student Sports Magazine* ranked Warren Harding the 15th best high school football team in the nation in 2002.

Thom was a former high-school baseball and football player at Orville High School in Orville, Ohio. He attended college at Ohio University before transferring to Clarion University in Clarion, Pennsylvania, where he received his degree in English. Coaching runs in the McDaniels family; Thom's son Josh is a defensive assistant football coach for the New England Patriots. Thom has coached hundreds of athletes who have received Division I scholarships all across the country, such as Ohio State, Michigan, University of Pittsburgh, and Michigan State to name just a few.

Three of Coach McDaniels' former players were on Ohio State's 2002 National Championship team and were all Big Ten selections: Kenny Peterson, defensive tackle who was a third-round draft pick of the Green Bay Packers; Michael Doss, a three-time All-American safety who was a second-round draft pick of the Indianapolis Colts; and Maurice Clarett, the *SPORTING NEWS* Freshman of the Year running back, who was *USA Today's* 2001 Offensive High-school Player of the Year.

Q: What advice do you have for high-school student athletes and their parents concerning the recruiting process that leads to athletic scholarships?

A: Many parents in communities all across the country become disappointed with their son or daughter's high-school coach because their child didn't receive a Division I scholarship. Listed below are ten questions we include in our monthly newsletter at Warren Harding High School that we send to our athletes and their parents. These are the 10 questions each player must ask to determine his worthiness to be offered and considered for a full athletic scholarship.

1. Do you have a 2.5 GPA in 14 core courses and have passed all proficiency tests?

2. Do you have an early ACT/SAT score that matches your core course GPA?

3. Do you meet the minimum requirements for major college football players in terms of height, weight, and speed by position?

4. Did you have a great season as a junior football player?

5. Did you have a great season as a senior football player?

6. Are you a good citizen with very few absences and tardies?

7. Will your head coach be able to tell recruiters that you have good work habits and a great, unselfish attitude?

8. Did your team have a great season your senior year?

9. Do your game films illustrate just how good a player you are?

10. Do you compare favorably to former Canton McKinley/Warren Harding athletes at your position who signed major college football scholarships?

College athletic departments are reluctant to invest $100,000 worth of free education in great high-school athletes who can not answer *"yes"* to those questions. More important, I am unwilling to promote a player who can't meet those standards—the worst thing a high school coach can do is to send a player to a school where he can't compete. *Honesty and forthrightness should never be mistaken for incompetence.* Recruiting is at best an exact science. It is far more complicated than the average guy on the street would ever believe.

Also included in our newsletter for the benefit of both our players and supporters is the *Ten Steps to a Winning Edge.*

Ten Steps To A Winning Edge

1. Are you coachable? Can you take criticism without looking for an alibi? Are you a know-it-all? Will you always try to improve?

2. Are you a positive team member? Do you contribute to team morale or do you bellyache and complain? Are you up when things go your way, down when they don't? Do you support your teammates and coaches or do you knock them?

3. Are you possessed with the spirit of competition that fires an intense desire to be successful? Do you never take "no" for an answer when there's a job to be done? Does it bother you to give less than 100 percent effort?

4. Are you mentally tough? When the going gets tough, do you get tougher? Do the screaming crowd or crucial situation shake you up—or make you rise to the challenge? Do you make excuses or do you suck it up and get the job done?

5. How are you under pressure? Can you concentrate on what needs to be done? Can you shut out of your mind a previous failure or personal insult and give special attention to the play that is happening here and now?

6. Do you have an ardent desire to improve? Are you eager to work diligently on your skills—especially those that need improvements?

7. Are you willing to practice? Do you just put in your time, or do you practice with the same intensity you bring into a game?

8. Are you willing to make sacrifices?

9. Are you willing to be impersonal toward your opponent? Do you shut out such feelings as fear and anger except to play hard as possible within the rules?

10. Are you willing to fulfill your responsibility as an athlete? Do you recognize that your attitude and actions–on and off the field– must be those of a class person representing a class program?

Q: When do you feel student athletes should be begin preparing for attending college and getting an education?

A: At the beginning of their ninth grade. This is when their grade point average begins.

Q: What do you feel separates the great athletes you have coached from the good athletes?

A: Attitude, Intelligence, and the ability to take criticism.

Q: What is your opinion on recruiting services who lead the athlete to believe that they will help them obtain an athletic scholarship?

A: I think that you would be throwing your money away.

Q: In light of the tragic death of the Minnesota Vikings Korey Stringer, who happened to be from Warren Harding High School, what is your opinion on supplements?

A: Stay away from them; there are no shortcuts to success!

Q: How has the collegiate athletic recruiting process changed in the last 10-20 years?

A: It is far more complicated than it used to be and it is ever changing. For example the NCAA's sliding scale has recently been changed, and the high-school student athlete must take 14 core courses for the 2003-04 school year rather than 13 that were required up until 2002-03 school year.

Q: What do you feel are the most important factors a high-school athlete needs to prepare for concerning the transition to playing sports in college?

A: 1.) Speed of the game. 2.) The competition is elevated. All the players on your college team were good in high school.

Q: What is it that you do personally as a coach and a friend that helps many of the athletes that you have coached in high school to be so prepared for college sports when they arrive on campus?

A: I have meetings with my athletes and their parents to inform them of

1.) what they need to do themselves,

2.) what the student athlete should consider when choosing a college,

3.) what they need to be realistically aware of concerning what college recruiters look for in a recruit, and

4.) how difficult the odds are of obtaining a scholarship.

I.) There are four forms that must be completed by student athletes and their parents. These forms cannot be filled out by a high-school coach.

These forms are

1. the transcript release form,

2. the clearinghouse form,

3. ACT / SAT registration form, and

4. FAFSA form,

II.) **This is the printout I provide for my student athletes to help them decide which college is the best fit for them.**

Choosing a college – Asking the right questions

1. **General Thoughts**

    A. Where should I go?
    B. What do I want to study?

2. **Education – Academics**

    A. What is the academic reputation of the school?

    B. Can I get the degree I want?

    C. Does the coaching staff emphasize academics?

    D. What is the graduation rate of football players at your school?

    E. Is there an academic plan for athletes?

    1. academic advisors
    2. tutoring
    3. mandatory study table
    4. preferred scheduling
    5. required class attendance

    F. Is summer school education part of the scholarship offer?

    G. Is a fifth year available if necessary to complete my degree?

3. **Head Coach – Assistant coaches**

    A. What is the national reputation of the head coach?

    B. What is the national reputation of the coaching staff?

    C. If I asked Coach McDaniels what kind of relationship he had with the coach who recruits Harding, what would he say?

D. If I asked Coach McDaniels if you and your coaches treated your players as people and students and not just football players, what would he say?

E. What is your general philosophy toward handling football players?

4. **The Athletic Scholarship (also called Grant-in-Aid)**

    A. What does the scholarship cover?

    B. Will I be offered a scholarship before my official visit or during my visit?

    C. Explain what the "National Letter of Intent" is.

    D. Is there a league or conference "letter of intent?"

5. **The College or University**

    A. Where is the school located? Is it rural, urban, or suburban setting?

    B. What is the distance from home?

    C. What are the campus, dormitories, and facilities like?

    D. What are the students like? What are the players like?

    E. Does the school have character, spirit, and tradition?

    F. Talk to me about the social aspects of the school.

       1. Will I fit in financially?

       2. Can I attend the church of my choice?

       3. What is the social climate of the school?

       4. What is the racial and ethnic balance of the student body?

6. **Other things to consider**

    A. What is the athletic tradition of the school? Are they a consistent winner? Are they rebuilding the program? Are they a regular bowl or playoff participant? Do they compete for the conference championship regularly?

    B. At what position am I being recruited?

    C. Can I compete when I am a sophomore?

    D. Is the head coach secure in his job? How long does he intend to be at this school?

    E. How long has he been there? Where else has he coached?

    F. How many returning players, lettermen, or starters are there at my position?

    G. How many other players are you recruiting at my position?

    H. How many scholarships are you offering this year?

    I. What are your offensive and defensive philosophies?

    J. What are the athletic facilities like?

        1. the stadium,
        2. the locker rooms,
        3. the practice areas, and
        4. the weight room and training rooms,

    K. What is the conference affiliation?

    L. What is your "red shirt" policy?

    M. How can this program help me reach my potential as a student and player?

N. Talk to me about the medical staff. What is your policy toward serious injury or career ending injury?

O. Is there media exposure?

P. Has there been any history of NCAA probation or investigation?

Q. Is there a mandatory drug testing policy presently in place?

7. **Things to remember**

   A. Eliminate from consideration any school that encourages you to cancel other visits.

   B. Be skeptical of coaches or recruiters who criticize other college programs.

   C. *You choose the college!* Ignore advice from friends, relatives, boosters, college alumni, or others. Consult with your parents. Ask for help from your high-school coach if necessary.

   D. Ask questions. There is no such thing as a "dumb question."

III.) **I provide the student athletes and their parents with the latest available information concerning the major college requirements by position for height, weight, and speed as well as a listing of testing averages from the National Football Leagues scouting combine.**

MAJOR COLLEGE REQUIREMENTS

OFFENSE	DEFENSE
WR	**DE**
6'0 172 Smallest	6'2 220 Smallest
6'5 220 Largest	6'6 260 Largest
6'2 190 Average	6'4 245 Average
4.4 - 4.5 Forty	4.6 – 4.9 Forty
TE	**DT**
6'2 220 Smallest	6'2 230 Smallest
6'6 250 Largest	6'6 270 Largest
6'4 240 Average	6'4 250 Average
4.7 – 4.9 Forty	4.9 – 5.2 Forty
OT	**1 Tech**
6'2 250 Smallest	5'11 215 Smallest
6'7 330 Largest	6'4 260 Largest
6'4 270 Average	6'2 245 Average
5.0 – 5.4 Forty	4.6 – 5.0 Forty
OG	**LB**
6'2 240 Smallest	6'0 200 Smallest
6'5 290 Largest	6'5 255 Largest
6'3 250 Average	6'3 225 Average
4.9 – 5.2 Forty	4.6 – 4.9 Forty
OC	**CORNER**
6'2 230 Smallest	5'9 170 Smallest
6'6 270 Largest	6'3 215 Largest
6'3 250 Average	6'2 195 Average
5.0 – 5.3 Forty	4.4 – 4.6 Forty

QB

6'0 175 Smallest
6'6 250 Largest
6'3 200 Average
4.6 – 4.9 Forty

FB

5'11 220 Smallest
6'4 260 Largest
6'3 240 Average
4.7 – 4.9 Forty

TB

5'8 175 Smallest
6'4 250 Largest
6'1 210 Average
4.5 – 4.6 Forty

FS / SS

6'0 180 Smallest
6'4 220 Largest
6'2 200 Average
4.5 – 4.8 Forty

Coach McDaniels goes over the game plan with his *USA TODAY* nationally ranked 2002 Warren Harding High School team prior to the state championship game in Canton, Ohio.

The following listings are the averages on the tests given by position from the 2002 NFL Combine

Many major college recruiters nowadays are looking for recruits whom they can project as future NFL players. I try to provide as much information as possible for my players and their parents so that they are realistically aware of what major college coaches are searching for in a potential recruit.

QUARTERBACKS

The average size of the quarterbacks was 6'2, 221 pounds (The bench press was not tested for quarterbacks)

10 yard Dash - (Average 1.68)
20 yard Dash - (Average 2.77)
40 yard Dash – (Average 4.80)
20y Shuttle – (Average 4.18)
Three Cone – (Average 7.10)
Vertical Jump – (Average 32.5)
Broad Jump – (Average 9'2")

RUNNING BACKS

The average size of the running backs was 5'11, 215 pounds

10 yard Dash – (Average 1.62)
20 yard Dash – (Average 2.68)
40 yard Dash – (Average 4.61)
20y Shuttle – (Average 4.18)
Three Cone – (Average 7.08)
Vertical Jump – (Average 35")
Broad Jump – (Average 9'8")
225 lb. Bench Press – (Average 19)

WIDE RECEIVERS

The average size of the receivers was 6', 198 pounds. (The bench press was not tested for wide receivers)

10 yard Dash – (Average 1.60)
20 yard Dash – (Average 2.61)
40 yard Dash – (Average 4.51)
20y Shuttle – (Average 3.76)
Three Cone - (Average 6.92)
Vertical Jump - (Average 36.5)
Broad Jump – (Average 10'1")

TIGHT ENDS

The average size of the tight ends was 6'4", 256 pounds.

10 yard Dash – (Average 1.71)
20 yard Dash – (Average 2.79)
40 yard Dash – (Average 4.81)
20y Shuttle – (Average 4.25)
Three Cone – (Average 7.19)
Vertical Jump – (Average 33")
Broad Jump – (Average 9'5")
225 lb. Bench Press – (Average 19)

CENTERS

The average size of the centers was 6'3", 265 pounds

10 yard Dash – (Average 1.75)
20 yard Dash – (Average 2.91)
40 yard Dash – (Average 5.07)
20y Shuttle – (Average 4.50)
Three Cone – (Average 7.51)
Vertical Jump – (Average 32")
Broad Jump – (Average 8'10")
225 lb. Bench Press – (Average 28)

GUARDS

The average size of the guards was 6'4", 317 pounds

10 yard Dash – (Average 1.85)
20 yard Dash – (Average 3.07)
40 yard Dash – (Average 5.35)
20y Shuttle – (Average 4.85)
Three Cone – (Average 8.13)
Vertical Jump – (Average 27.5")
Broad Jump – (Average 8'3")
225 lb. Bench Press – (Average 26)

TACKLES (OFFENSE)

The average size of the tackles was 6'6", 320 pounds

10 yard Dash – (Average 1.84)
20 yard Dash – (Average 3.04)
40 yard Dash – (Average 5.30)
20y Shuttle – (Average 4.75)
Three Cone – (Average 7.89)
Vertical Jump – (Average 29")
Broad Jump – (Average 8'7")
225 lb. Bench Press – (Average 26)

TACKLES (DEFENSE)

The average size of the defensive tackles was 6'4", 302 pounds

10 yard Dash – (Average 1.77)
20 yard Dash – (Average 2.89)
40 yard Dash – (Average 5.08)
20y Shuttle – (Average 4.51)
Three Cone – (Average 7.59)
Vertical Jump – (Average 31")
Broad Jump – (Average 8'7")
225 lb. Bench Press – (Average 27)

DEFENSIVE ENDS

The average size of the defensive ends was 6'4", 270 pounds.

10 yard Dash – (Average 1.71)
20 yard Dash – (Average 2.79)
40 yard Dash – (Average 4.81)
20y Shuttle – (Average 4.34)
Three Cone – (Average 7.32)
Vertical Jump – (Average 34.5")
Broad Jump – (Average 9'5")
225 lb. Bench Press – (Average 25)

INSIDE LINEBACKERS

The average size of the inside linebackers was 6'3", 244 pounds.

10 yard Dash – (Average 1.70)
20 yard Dash – (Average 2.76)
40 yard Dash – (Average 4.80)
20y Shuttle – (Average 4.24)
Three Cone – (Average 7.08)
Vertical Jump – (Average 34")
Broad Jump – (Average 9'7")
225 lb. Bench Press – (Average 22)

OUTSIDE LINEBACKERS

The average size of the outside linebackers was 6'2", 241 pounds.

10 yard Dash – (Average 1.65)
20 yard Dash – (Average 2.70)
40 yard Dash – (Average 4.69)
20y Shuttle – (Average 4.23)
Three Cone – (Average 7.12)
Vertical Jump – (Average 35")
Broad Jump – (Average 9'9")
225 lb. Bench Press – (Average 23)

CORNERBACKS

The average size of the cornerbacks was 5'11", 193 pounds.

10 yard Dash – (Average 1.62)
20 yard Dash – (Average 2.63)
40 yard Dash – (Average 4.55)
20y Shuttle – (Average 4.18)
Three Cones – (Average 7.02)
Vertical Jump – (Average 37")
Broad Jump – (Average 10')
225 lb. Bench Press – (Average 14)

FREE SAFETIES

The average size of the free safeties was 6'1", 208 pounds.

10 yard Dash – (Average 1.62)
20 yard Dash – (Average 2.65)
40 yard Dash – (Average 4.59)
20y Shuttle – (Average 4.06)
Three Cones – (Average 6.99)
Vertical Jump – (Average 36")
Broad Jump – (Average 10'2")
225 lb. Bench Press – (Average 17)

STRONG SAFETIES

The average size of the strong safeties was 6', 211 pounds.

10 yard Dash – (Average 1.62)
20 yard Dash – (Average 2.66)
40 yard Dash – (Average 4.59)
20y Shuttle – (Average 4.08)
Three Cones – (Average 6.87)
Vertical Jump – (Average 35.5")
Broad Jump – (Average 10')
225 lb. Bench Press – (Average 21)

Advice from John Zizzo, Former Scout for the Colorado Rockies

John's background includes working as a former professional baseball scout for the Colorado Rockies and as a minor league coach in Bend, Oregon; Sioux Falls, South Dakota; and Canton, Ohio. He also was a college coach for Youngstown State University in Ohio. Currently, John is a personal instructor and the father of two high-school and one junior-high athletes, who now lives in Florida.

Q: As a former college recruiter, do you have any advice for high-school student athletes on the collegiate athletic recruiting process?

A: When deciding on which college you'll be attending to participate in sports, you should base your choices on the following:

1. Do you like and feel comfortable with the coach? Will this person be someone with whom you want to spend the next four years of your life?

2. Is the college that you'll be attending right for you—one where you'll be able to achieve your academic and athletic goals?

3. Are you aware of and did you research the type of team and the players on the team at the college you want to attend? Are there several players playing at your position already, and are they seniors or freshmen now?

Q: Do you have any advice for the parents of high-school athletes?

A: When you're helping in the decision of which college your son/daughter may attend, consider the following:

1. Do you also like the college coach and do you feel comfortable that this coach will guide him/her through his/her college years academically, athletically, and socially?

2. Have you and your child discussed all of the factors involved in the decision regarding the college's location? For example, will your child attend a college where you may not be able to visit him/her very often or at all or will he/she not be able to come home for a weekend because of the distance from home? You must discuss whether both parties will be able to handle this situation since parents want to visit and watch their children play as often as possible.

Q: Do you have any advice for junior-high student athletes?

A: Don't ever count yourself out of the possibilities of ever having the chance to pursue an athletic scholarship because of your size in your junior-high years. Many great athletes have physically developed slower than other athletes in their class grades. As you probably know, Michael Jordan didn't make the varsity basketball team in his sophomore year in high-school and went on to become one of the greatest basketball players of all time. Bobby Jones, who also is interviewed in this guide, was only 5'3" and 110 lbs. in 9th grade but kept believing in himself as an athlete and went on to play in the NFL for seven years as a wide receiver. The bottom line is: *If you don't believe in yourself, then you shouldn't expect anybody else to believe in you.*

Q: As a former professional scout and coach, what did you look for in a prospect?

A: Prospects are evaluated on whether they have certain tools and what kind of personal makeup they have. The five tools baseball players are evaluated on are

1. speed, 2. if they can hit for average, 3. if they can hit for power, 4. arm strength, and 5. if they can field their position and how many positions they can play.

When it comes to personal makeup, the scout must determine whether this prospect has a good work ethic, if he/she is coachable, if he/she hustles and plays hard all of the time, and if he/she loves and respects the game. There are many factors involved in the personal makeup of the prospect, and many times if the prospect has at least three of these tools, the personal makeup will be the deciding factor on whether he/she is drafted or signs to a professional contract.

Q: Do you have any advice for high-school student athletes who are offered a professional contract out of high school?

A: You have to consider many factors before making such a decision:

1. Finances: Will you be receiving enough money to pay for your college education with the contract you'll receive, or will the contract include the organization paying for your college education? You must have something to fall back on if you get injured or released in the future.

2. Maturity: Will you be able to handle going directly into an adult life-style environment where the majority of players will be several years older and wiser than you?

3. Do you understand that if you do plan to attend college to play that sport, you'll have to wait until after your junior year is over to be drafted again? The exception is enrolling in a junior college where you could be drafted after your first or second year in junior college.

   There are many factors to consider before making such an important decision; make sure you discuss all of them with your parents instead of making a quick decision. *Information is power!*

John with Gary DeNiro (R), a former linebacker who played on two University of Alabama national championship football teams.

Advice from Russ Hake,
High-school Football and Baseball Coach,
Former College Halfback

Russ is currently a 20-year veteran high-school head baseball coach with 30 years' experience as a high-school football coach. He was a three-year starter as a halfback at Girard High School, Girard, Ohio, and three-year starter at halfback at Murray State University in Kentucky. Numerous athletes that Russ has coached have received baseball or football scholarships to colleges such as Arizona, Ohio State, Michigan, Penn State, Ohio University, West Virginia, Akron, Pittsburgh, and Notre Dame.

Q: Can you explain for student athletes and parents what is the college coach's point of view concerning the business side of the athletic recruiting process?

A: For coaches and high school athletes, it should be looked at as a business. The coach needs to win or it's his job. For the high-school athlete, it should be "Where is the best place for me?" You could be a fringe player at best at the major Division I schools but a starter at Division 1AA, II, or III. Getting the *degree* is the *key*!

Q: What do you suggest that student athletes do to determine which division level is best suited for them to participate in?

A: Young people often don't look at things realistically nor do their parents. Ask your coach where the best place is for you. You don't want to look back at your college days and say, "I played four years at a Division I college and was a great scout player," when you could say you played at a lower division level school and *started*.

Q: What do you suggest that student athletes do to get noticed?

A: If you need to promote yourself, you aren't a top level player in most cases.

Q: **How do college coaches determine the amount of heart and desire a student athlete has?**

A: It's a tough business and it's not easy. It's a skill that people have. Talk to a person for awhile, and you find out a lot. Then check high school coaches, teachers, etc.

Q: **What's your opinion on sports camps? Should student athletes attend them?**

A: Go and have fun; you might learn a thing or two but never put a camp ahead of your team's practice. You'll meet coaches and other good athletes at camps.

Q: **Do you think you need to know someone, be lucky, or get a break to get an athletic scholarship?**

A: If you're good, you'll be noticed. The question is: Does the coach think you're someone who fits into his/her program needs?

Q: **Do you think you have to come from a big school to get an athletic scholarship?**

A: I think the big schools get more attention, but they know there are "diamonds in the rough" [at small schools].

Q: **What do college coaches look for when they're recruiting besides size, speed, and strength?**

A: *Team player*! Is he going to go to class and make the effort to pass? Is he going to stay out of trouble? A college scholarship is an investment the coach makes. If the coach makes too many bad investments, he's out of a job.

Q: **Do you have any advice for the parents on the athletic recruiting process?**

A: *Be realistic*! Make the four years a good and memorable experience for your child. For example, if he plays football, you don't want him to be a "blocking dummy" on the scout squad for four years when he can possibly be playing for another college that may be a lower division level.

Q: **How important is a professional appearance when speaking to college recruiters? (For examples, things like earrings, tattoos, hats on backwards, dyed hair, etc.)**

A: Recruiters are businessmen. Approach the meeting as a job interview because it is! Cover your tattoos, take out the earrings, get the natural look. You're giving a first impression for a college education, not a job interview with Barnum & Bailey Circus!

Q: **Do you have any advice for junior-high student athletes?**

A: Yes. Go out for the team so you can have a successful team with your childhood friends. This is the best of times. Work hard and *have fun*!

Q: **Do you feel that there is an exact step-by-step process that a high-school athlete can follow that guarantees an athletic scholarship?**

A: If you follow a step-by-step proces to get an athletic scholarship, you are guaranteed nothing! I think that the college coach first wants to know if the student athletes can help the college's program, if they can make an impact, if they can get into the college and progress academically, and what behavior issues have to be questioned. If you can't play on that level, nothing else will matter.

Coach Hake (L) gives some pitching advice to the author during his high-school playing days.

Q: Do you have any other advice or information you would like to share with today's student athletes?

A: I want all young athletes to know that participating in sports will be beneficial to them later in life, regardless of whether they receive an athletic scholarship or not. Sure, it would be nice for youngsters to be rewarded with an athletic scholarship for all of the time and hard work they put into their sport, but there is much more to participating in sports. Participating in sports will develop character, build friendships that last a lifetime, and help to deal with the challenges and obstacles that will arise during their days as an adult.

A fellow coach and a very good friend of mine, John Delserone, is an excellent example of how participating in high-school sports builds character. He was the head coach of our Brookfield High School's 1978 State Championship high-school football team and the "AA Coach of the Year in Ohio." He was a special individual who would go to great lengths to help youngsters become better people, not just better student athletes. What made John so special was that he had the ability to be stern, sensitive, and understanding at the same time, both on and off the field. John had the ability to motivate his players to be the best players they could possibly be, at the same time keeping them loose and making them aware that the game they were playing was simply that—just a game. *"Playing a game regardless of the outcome is not a life or death situation,"* Coach Delserone would say. He motivated his players by telling them to "play each game as if it were their last because you never know what may happen to you on or off the field."

Unfortunately, John had to use some of his own advice because shortly after our championship season, he was suddenly stricken by Lou Gehrig's disease. John loved helping youngsters and coaching so much that he refused to give in to the disease that gradually ate at his body. John knew that he had to be strong if he expected his players, coaches, family, and friends to be strong too.

Instead of giving into this incurable disease that would have kept a normal person from leaving his house, John found the strength and courage to coach our high-school football team from a wheelchair in the press box. Coach Delserone lost almost all of his ability to communicate. His only means of communicating was by pointing or by blinking his eyes. We had an assistant coach standing next to Coach Delserone with a prearranged selection of plays. This coach interpreted the instructions he received and relayed the play to another coach on the sideline. John was our inspirational leader even in the condition he was in because he refused to quit doing what he loved to do the most—helping young athletes become better players and people.

Coach Delserone applied much of what he acquired from playing and coaching high-school sports into real-life situations. It is impossible for me, any of the other assistant coaches, or the players on the team to explain the magnitude of the impact this special man had on all of our lives. Through his actions while fighting an incurable disease, he was able to show our entire community just how valuable participating in sports was to him, a former high-school athlete, even one who didn't get an athletic scholarship.

Coach Delserone remained strong-minded even while confined to a bed, as evidenced by his being able to write a book with an assistant who interpreted his words through blinking his eyes. Each and every one of us throughout the entire high-school and community was fortunate to meet a man like John—the epitome of courage. He showed us just how valuable participating in sports was and how he was able to apply skills that he had acquired from playing and coaching into handling real-life situations.

Coach Hake (far left) with assistant football coaches Tim Flipovich, Joe Donofrio, Walt Nogay, Dan Deramo, and John Delserone, head coach of the Brookfield High School 1978 Ohio State Championship team.

Advice from Dan Deramo, High-school Football/Girls' Volleyball Coach, A. D.

Dan has been the girls' head volleyball coach at Brookfield High School in Ohio for 13 years, as well as a Junior Olympic volleyball coach for six years. He was an assistant football coach for the State Championship football team and the athletic director. As a high-school student, he was a starter for three years as a guard and linebacker for Girard High School, Girard, Ohio. Dan attended Heidelberg College in Ohio, where he earned a degree in math education. Currently, he is an 8th grade math teacher in the Brookfield school system, where he's been a teacher and coach for 27 years. Dan has coached athletes who have received Division I football scholarships to colleges such as Arizona, Michigan, Ohio State, Penn State, Kent State, and West Virginia.

Q: **As a coach for both boys' football and then girls' volleyball, do you feel there's any difference when it comes to the collegiate athletic recruiting process between genders?**

A: Not really. I think because of football, the boys' recruiting process is more publicized, but if a college wants a player—male or female— it will use every recruiting tool possible to get that player.

Q: **How do you suggest that the female student athlete who plays volleyball go about getting noticed and promoting herself to college recruiters?**

A: Send videotapes of your matches to colleges. Attend summer camps at colleges, and play Junior Olympic volleyball.

Q: **What advice do you have for the student athlete and parents when it comes to deciding on which colleges they should market themselves to?**

A: Attend a college you'll be comfortable with even if you don't play athletics. The main reason you're going to college is to get an education and a degree.

Q: Do you have any advice for female or male junior-high student athletes who aspire to participate in collegiate or professional sports some day?

A: Develop good study habits for the classroom and good practice habits for the field of play. Learn to accept teaching and coaching and continually strive to improve your skills in all areas—especially your weak areas.

Q: Do you think a female student athlete has to come from a large high school to receive an athletic scholarship?

A: *No!* If you're good enough, they'll find you.

Q: Do you think that high-school student athletes increase their chances of becoming noticed and recruited if they participate in additional programs for their sport during the off-season versus just playing their sport during their school's high-school season?

A: *Absolutely!* The Junior Olympic volleyball program is a great example of this.

Q: Do you feel it's harder for a female student athlete to get an athletic scholarship than for a male?

A: Not really. Many colleges are looking to expand their female athletic programs, thus creating more opportunities for females. The so-called "minor" sports of volleyball, softball, and gymnastics are always looking for good student athletes for their institutions.

Coach Deramo with his 2000 Brookfield High School girls' volleyball team that went 20-5 and was district champion and regional qualifier.

HARD LUCK STORIES

THE

"REALITY OF SPORTS"

Advice from Marcus Marek, Two-time OSU All-American Linebacker

Photo by Marc Jablonski

Marcus was an All-Ohio linebacker for the state champion Brookfield Warriors in high school, a two-time All-American, and the all time career-leading tackler in Ohio State history. Marcus recently was inducted into the Ohio State Athletic Hall of Fame. He also played professionally for three years in the USFL for the Portland, New Orleans, and Boston Breakers and then briefly for the Cleveland Browns and Chicago Bears before suffering a career-ending injury.

Q: What advice do you have for junior-high athletes and their parents?

A: As a parent of four children myself, I personally do not want my children playing on their computer for more than 45 minutes a day. I tell them to go outside and *be active*, find something to do or play. Go outside even if you are going to just sit and enjoy the outdoors.

Q: What advice do you have for the "blue chip" athlete who has to decide on whether to attend a college where there is or will be a change of head coaches?

A: I had the personal experience of having to deal with the changing of coaches who were recruiting me in my senior year in high school (Woody Hayes at first until the last game of that season for OSU and then the waiting period before Earle Bruce was hired that winter; another example is the recent transition from John Cooper to Jim Tressel at OSU).

If the student athlete is seriously interested in attending a college with circumstances such as this, first of all, I suggest he/she visit the campus and sports facilities even if the college hasn't decided on a coach to see if he/she really wants to attend that university. In the case of visiting Ohio State, you'll be so impressed by the quality of the sports program, the campus, and the tradition of the school that you'll want to play with them regardless of who the coach is or will be. You can be assured that the university will select a qualified coach for its sports program.

Q: **What was the toughest situation you ever faced as an athlete?**

A: It was in Ann Arbor, Michigan, without a doubt, that as a freshman, I had to try to call the defensive signals against the Michigan Wolverines in front of 106,000 screaming fans.

Marcus (L) with the Ohio State assistant coach who recruited him, Glen Mason, at an Ohio State football banquet. Mason is now the head football coach at the University of Minnesota and president of the American Football Coaches' Association.

Author's note: *For you athletes out there, Marcus Marek's story is a prime example of how difficult it is to make it to the NFL, even with all of the accomplishments and awards he received for his performance at Ohio State. He was still considered too small (6"2', 215 lbs.) to play linebacker in the NFL. He even played three years in the USFL at that time (a league that was very close to the NFL talentwise) and made the All-USFL team. His outstanding performance there also still wasn't good enough for many NFL teams to consider him as a future NFL player. By the time he did get a chance to play in the NFL, he had to overcome some serious injuries that ultimately led to his retirement from football.*

I grew up playing baseball, football, and basketball since Little League with Marcus, and he was, by far, the most competitive player I ever had the pleasure of playing with or against. NFL scouts and coaches knew this, too. His coach from Ohio State, Earle Bruce, puts him in a special category of players that he has ever coached.

This story is the reality of just how difficult it can be to make it to the NFL. Marcus was smart enough to get his college education in case something unforeseen happened to his football career. He is now the owner of a lobster company in New Hampshire.

Marcus recovers a fumble against the University of Iowa.

Photo taken by Marc Jablonski

Marcus Marek is ready for action during his playing days as linebacker for the Ohio State Buckeyes.

Advice from Andy Timko, Baltimore Orioles' 3rd-Round Pick

Andy was a two-sport star in baseball and basketball at Warren JFK High School in Ohio. He received a baseball scholarship to attend Alabama University on the advice of a prominent baseball scout. The Alabama coach had never seen him play. Alabama was so interested in recruiting Andy that they even had the legendary football coach Paul "Bear" Bryant, one of the winningest football coaches of all time, handle the signing of his Letter of Intent. Shortly after the scholarship offer, Andy was drafted as a shortstop in the 3rd round of the baseball draft by the Baltimore Orioles. He decided to sign the professional baseball contract because he was picked so high in the draft. That usually means that great things are expected of an athlete by the organization that chooses so high and that they'll invest a nice sum of money as a bonus.

Andy played for five years in the Baltimore minor league system and had an excellent career batting average of .300 before retiring. Nobody ever could have predicted that the other shortstop who was drafted in the 2nd round the previous year would have produced as well as he did. That shortstop also played in the minors at the same time Andy did and then got the first shot at the starting job for the Orioles. He went on to become the Rookie of the Year in his first year and the American League's Most Valuable Player the next year. Andy waited patiently for his break to come for several years. This other shortstop never missed a game the entire time Andy was waiting in the wings. Andy finally decided to retire after deciding that the other guy would never get hurt and miss a game.

Andy wasn't wrong—well, at least he wasn't wrong for the next 14 years about this shortstop never missing a game. The shortstop had already won another Most Valuable Player award and two Gold Gloves awards and was selected to start a Major League record of 16 straight all-star games. The shortstop finally asked his manager to sit him down after playing 2,632 consecutive games—a span of over 16 straight years. That shortstop's name is *Cal Ripken*!

Q: If you have the chance to do it all over again, would you do anything differently?

A: I have no regrets about my choice to sign a professional baseball contract rather than taking the scholarship offer to the University of Alabama. I enjoyed a very good career in baseball while I played, and it was a very good contract that I received from the Orioles because of the round I was drafted in.

But! If I had the chance to do it again, I definitely would have gone to Alabama on a baseball scholarship, not only to get my education but also to play on the UA baseball team. They had a great team with guys like Dave Magadan and company, and they went on to win the National Championship during that time. In hindsight, I possibly could have been drafted by another organization other than the Orioles the next time I was eligible for the draft, and I'm sure it would have been a much different situation than the one in which I was involved with Cal Ripken and the Orioles.

There's no way of ever predicting or knowing what's in store for you in your future, but you could have a good idea of what might be ahead if you go to college and get your education. *Andy earned a degree in business from Youngstown State University after his baseball career was over.*

1980 Bonus Babies: Andy, 3rd-round draft pick, with 1st-round draft pick, Jeff Williams (L), prior to a Rookie League game in Bluefield, Virginia.

Advice from Jim Winterburn, All-American High-school Baseball Player

Jim's background includes being selected as a high-school All- American while playing baseball for Austintown Fitch High School in Ohio, where he was a standout performer in basketball and football, as well. He received a baseball scholarship to the University of Akron. Currently, he is a junior high track coach in Youngstown, Ohio.

Between seriously injuring his shoulder and not liking the living conditions at Akron, he decided, on the advice of the Ohio University coach, to attend OU and to try out as a walk-on. His try-out experience left him feeling that the coach hadn't been totally honest with him the previous year when he'd talked about his chances of playing on a team. He felt that the coach wasn't convinced that Jim's shoulder had completely healed. He decided to hang up his cleats and concentrate solely on his studies, moving on in his career by getting his college education in marketing.

Jim's story is not unlike that of many youngsters who grew up eating, drinking, and sleeping sports and dreaming of becoming a professional sports star. In Jim's case, he envisioned being a professional sports star in whatever sport was in season at the time. He had such high hopes and dreams that he even practiced giving interviews for his future sports career in front of a mirror while holding the ball of the sport that was in season.

Even though Jim was a great baseball player before his shoulder injury, coaches didn't see him as the same prospect because of the injury and were afraid to take the chance of "wasting a scholarship." Coaches view scholarships as an investment in not only the school but also in their own future personal situations. Not only do coaches have to answer to athletic directors and other superiors about why they give a scholarship to an injured player, but they also have to consider their own win-loss records.

Jim never gave up on his dreams—he just realized that his dreams were no longer realistically obtainable because of his injury. He was mature enough to move on with his life and concentrate on getting his college education. He knew inside that he had given sports his best shot and now has no regrets about retiring without ever playing in a college game, even though he was selected All-American in high school.

His advice to junior- and senior-high student athletes and their parents is to have as much fun playing sports for as long as they can because no one ever knows when that game may be the last!

He strongly suggests that student athletes concentrate on getting their college education to have something to fall back on in case an injury occurs. The first step to getting a scholarship is hitting the books hard, beginning in 9th grade, which will be measured as important as senior grades. The accumulated grade point average will show the colleges your commitment to education.

Q: How did the injury to your shoulder happen that hurt your chances of playing college and professional baseball?

A: The injury to my shoulder happened when I was playing 9th grade football. I was quarterback and running an option play when I was leveled by the defensive end. That hit to my shoulder kept me from playing quarterback the rest of my football career. I had to play halfback from then on. The injury also ended my days as a pitcher.

The injury to my shoulder gradually got worse over the years and caused my throwing arm (as a shortstop) to weaken. My injury didn't affect my hitting in baseball but it did affect my throwing. Although my arm was good enough to get by with as a high-school baseball player, it wasn't good enough to play that position in college, so I had to play first base. Because I had the build of a middle infielder (5' 10" - 180 lbs.), I was never taken seriously as a potential first baseman. Typically, a college first baseman stand well over six feet tall and weighs well over 200 lbs.

Q: Is there any other advice you would like to offer today's young athletes?

A: I would like to let young athletes know that to get athletic scholarships, they don't have to be star athletes receiving all of the attention on the teams that they played on in junior and senior high school. Some youngsters develop later than others, and in some situations, it may just take a special coach who sees something in a youngster that nobody else sees and, therefore, takes the time to help that athlete become a better player.

An excellent example of this is Mike Trgovac, the defensive coordinator for the Carolina Panthers and one of my best friends in high school. Mike didn't start on his freshman or sophomore football teams. Then something happened one day at practice, and our defensive line coach, Bob Stoops, saw something special in Mike, who was playing fullback at the time, and took him under his wing.

Within the next two years under coach Stoops' tutelage, Mike ended up becoming an All-State defensive lineman and was selected as the "most valuable player of the game" in Ohio's North-South high-school all-star game. Mike was also the state wrestling champion in the heavyweight division his senior year.

Mike was heavily recruited by major colleges all across the country before deciding to attend the University of Michigan on a football scholarship, where he went on to become an All-American even though he didn't start on his junior-high or junior-varsity football teams.

Jim (R) with his son Jimmy (L), and high-school teammate Mike Trgovac, Carolina Panthers defensive coordinator and University of Michigan All-American, at the Curbstone Coaches Hall of Fame Banquet in Youngstown, Ohio.

Advice from Al Gonzales, All-American H. S. Baseball Player

As a 12-year-old Little Leaguer in 7th grade, Al threw several no-hitters. After striking out all 18 batters in an All-Star game, his picture and an article about his incredible feat were published in a *Sports Illustrated*'s section called "Faces in the Crowd." Imagine having millions of people across the country knowing about you while you're still in junior high!

At 18, Al was an All-American baseball player for his Austintown Fitch High School team in Ohio. Soon after his high school season was over, so was his career because Al seriously injured his throwing arm and could no longer pitch at the level he had previously done.

He was overused as a pitcher throughout his brief career because he was so good. His injury came simply by not having enough rest between the games he pitched in his career.

When asked about his feelings about the injury that ended his career, Al said, "That's life! What can you do about it?"

Q: What advice do you have for parents of young athletes?

A: Be sure that your young athletes realize that they need to have something to fall back on—a college education when their playing days are over.

Q: What advice do you have for student athletes of all ages?

A: Play each game with as much enthusiasm as you can because you never know when your last game will be.

Q: How did the injury to your throwing arm happen that hurt your chances of playing college and professional baseball?

A: To be honest, I never actually had an injury that caused my throwing arm to weaken. To make a long story short, I was the ace of our high school pitching staff that made it to the Ohio State championship game my senior year. I was 15-0 and had pitched in well over half of our games that season. We finished 29-2, our team was on a roll and we kept winning all of our tournament playoff games and I thought my arm could handle all the pitching that I was doing. My arm felt fine and because it was so much fun winning, I kept telling the coach I could pitch even if I had just pitched in a ball game a day or two before.

The bottom line is that I had pitched too much too often that spring, and my arm was shot once the dust had settled from our fantastic run through the state tournament games. I actually never suffered an injury that hurt my arm, and I never felt the pain in my arm. I simply lost the majority of the velocity I had on my fastball because I overused my arm pitching.

Q: Would you do anything different if you had the chance to do it again?

A: In hindsight, it would be easy to say I should have rested my arm more and not pitched so often. But how do you as an 18-year-old tell your coach or your teammates that you can't pitch in the biggest games of all of our lives at that point in time even though your arm feels fine? I guess I should have realized I was pitching too much or the coach should have told me it just wasn't wise for me to be pitching so much because it could hurt my arm in the long run. I can't blame the coach because I told him my arm felt fine and I wanted to pitch.

Al with fellow high-school All-American teammate Jim Winterburn (L).

Advice from Bill Sattler, Former Expos Pitcher

Bill was signed as a free agent by the Montreal Expos. He played professionally for six years in the minor leagues, and three of those years were at the AAA level, one step below the major leagues. At Woodrow Wilson High School in Youngstown, Ohio, Bill was a standout pitcher and later received a scholarship to play baseball at Youngstown State University.

Currently, he's the head baseball coach at Columbiana High School in Ohio and also coaches for the Astro Falcon Baseball Organization's summer league team in Struthers, Ohio. In addition, Bill is an Ohio State Highway patrolman.

Q: What do you suggest is the best way for a high-school student athlete to be noticed?

A: As far as baseball goes, I feel that the better the competition a young athlete plays against, the better his/her chances become of getting noticed. Many times, an athlete is fortunate enough to be noticed by college recruiters while playing against somebody on another team who's being watched.

Q: What advice do you have for high-school student athletes and their parents concerning the athletic recruiting process and college scholarships?

A: Student athletes and their parents all need to realize how difficult it is to get an athletic scholarship. The actual percentages of high school athletes who receive athletic scholarships are much lower than you might be aware of, and the odds of becoming a professional athlete later on are even smaller.

Q: What advice do you have for junior-high athletes and their parents?

A: You must understand that many players can be good when they're in Little League because there are many more teams and players at that level. But as players get older, the number of teams and players decrease while at the same time, the competition increases.

Author's note: *Bill played exceptionally well for three years at the AAA level, and one season, he even had the best earned-run average in the entire AAA league he performed in. Regardless of how well he did at that level, he still was never called up to the major league team. I asked Bill why he thought he was never given the chance to play at the major league level when he did so well in the minors. He said that the Expos' organization simply didn't feel he was big enough to pitch at that level, and they wanted their pitchers to be taller than Bill was—5'11" and 165 lbs.*

For you young athletes out there: This is just another example of how hard it is to make it to the major leagues. What more could Bill have done? He performed well enough, as evidenced by his statistics, to deserve a chance to play in the majors, but he couldn't will himself to grow taller.

Sattler warms up in the bullpen for a Monteal Expo's spring traing game with West Palm Beach, Florida.

Advice from Don Christian, Walk-on Pitcher at Tulane

Don is a former walk-on pitcher for the nationally ranked Tulane University's Green Wave of New Orleans, Louisiana. Currently, he's director of the Astro Falcons Baseball Organization, located at Bob Cene Park baseball complex in Struthers, Ohio, the home of the Youngstown Class "B" league. Don played football in high school and once pitched back-to-back no-hitters for his Poland High Bulldogs baseball team from Poland, Ohio.

Q: Do you have any advice for the student athlete who plans to try out as a walk-on at a major university?

A: Don't be afraid to try out as a walk-on. I still believe the serious baseball player has a better shot at being noticed by a professional organization at a big-time program than he or she would ever be at a Division II or III school.

Q: Why did you try out as a walk-on for Tulane, who was a national power at that time (and still is)?

A: My high school started baseball only in my senior year, so I didn't get much exposure. Pro scouts encouraged me to either go South or out West for college. If you're serious about baseball, Ohio doesn't have the best spring weather. I wanted to go South and to a small school. Tulane in Louisiana had only 5,000 students, so I chose to walk on there.

Q: Would you do anything differently if you had the chance to do it again?

A: My biggest mistake was coming back too soon after I injured my knee in college. I just couldn't wait to play, and my knee wasn't strong enough. The next injury totally destroyed my knee.

Q: What are the advantages of trying out for a college sport as a walk-on?

A: College teams are limited on the number of scholarships and coaches need walk-ons to finish their teams.

Q: What are some of the disadvantages of trying out for a college sport as a walk-on?

A: Most college coaches figure if they already have you as a walk-on, they never have to use any of their scholarship money on you. You almost have to beg or threaten to leave school to ever receive any aid.

Q: What are some of the disadvantages of being a walk-on who has made a college team, and how is a walk-on player treated in comparison to a scholarship athlete?

A: My coach admitted to me that I was a better pitcher than some scholarship players, but he was forced to start them or he'd lose his job. He made me a short reliever to come in to bail out some of his scholarship players.

Q: With all of your experience of being a player, coach, and now the parent of a student athlete, what advice do you have on collegiate athletic recruiting experience for high-school student athletes?

A: Look closely at the coach. Is he/she the person you want to spend the next four years with? Talk with walk-on athletes. They don't owe the coach anything, and they tend to be more honest.

Q: How about junior-high athletes?

A: Develop good practice habits, work hard, try harder.

Q: And what about parents?

A: Don't listen to promises. A coach may be one of the most influential people in your child's life. Choose one wisely.

Q: What are the most important factors that you believe student athletes should be aware of in the transition from high school to the collegiate sports level?

A: In high school, sports are a game. In college, a coach makes a living for his family by coaching. It's a business at the college level, no matter which division you choose.

Q: Do you feel a student athlete's chances of being recruited increase if college coaches know he/she will be receiving academic money for college because of maintaining a high GPA?

A: Because of scholarship limitations, academic grants are a coach's best friend. In all divisions, no coach wants a player who can't stay eligible or who flunks out.

Q: What do you suggest that student athletes do to get noticed and recruited?

A: Most coaches love to watch the player practice more than play. If you're on the field, always try your best.

Q: What do you suggest is the best way for student athletes to find out what division level is best suited for their athletic and academic abilities?

A: At Tulane, I played with Brian Martiny, who was a first-team All-American. As a center fielder, Brian had good games against Miami University of Florida, whose coach was the legendary Ron Frasier. (South Alabama's coach Eddie Stanky was also a legend.) Their votes carried a lot of clout. Was Brian Martiny the best outfielder in the country? All I can say personally is that I've played with better players locally than he was, Jim Hamrock, for example, but Martiny was in the right place at the right time.

What I'm trying to convey is that sports is a very arbitrary subject! A coach at one division level may see you as a prospect, where another coach at the same division may not. *Don't sell yourself short!* My advice is to keep in mind that you're attending college to get an education first of all, so you should consider what field of education you're interested in and try to match a campus and a college sports program that will be best suited for you.

Author's note: *Don Christian and his father, Bill, were the only coaches who believed that I could play baseball in a league of basically 17-18-year-olds when I was a skinny 15-year-old high-school sophomore. The experience of playing against older and better competition at that age was a tremendous learning experience for me at that point in my life. It was one that led me not only to mature and get better that year but also to receive a baseball scholarship to Ohio University the very next year at only age 16. Don is now in charge of that very same league I played in—the Youngstown Class "B" League at the Astro Falcon Baseball Complex at Bob Cene Field, Struthers, Ohio.*

Coach Christian gives some tips on proper pitching mechanics to a young ballplayer.

Advice from Todd Santore, Fresh Out of College

Todd's background includes receiving a baseball scholarship and being selected as an All-Midwestern Collegiate Conference catcher for the Youngstown State Penguins, Youngstown, Ohio, in the 2001 season. His lifetime batting average was .345 during his collegiate days. Currently, he's working for the Astro Falcon Baseball Organization and completing work for his B. S. in Criminal Justice at YSU.

Q: What advice do you have for high-school student athletes on the collegiate athletic recruiting process?

A: Play as many sports as you can in high school, enjoy your high-school sports experiences, and get your education so that you have something to fall back on if you get hurt.

Q: What advice do you have for parents on the recruiting process?

A: My advice to parents is the same as my parents gave me and that is to make sure you have something to fall back on in case you don't make it professionally for whatever reason it may be—injury or not making the grade athletically.

Q: What advice do you have for junior-high student athletes?

A: Have fun playing sports while learning your game. Enjoy your youth.

Q: Looking back, was there anything you would have done differently in your athletic career?

A: I regret the fact that I concentrated on only one sport in high school—baseball. Looking back, I wish I'd have participated in football, too, which would have allowed me to enjoy my high-school sports experience better.

Q: What advice do you have for high-school student athletes about how to get themselves noticed?

A: Run the 60-yard dash in seven seconds or less if you play a fielding position, throw the ball over 90 miles per hour if you're a pitcher, grow tall if you're a catcher, play in the most competitive leagues, preferably wooden bat leagues if you're trying to make it to the professional level. If you're good, you'll be noticed, but so will many other ball players. If you can show them that you're a faster runner or can throw harder than another player, you'll increase your chances of getting noticed.

Q: Do you feel that if your statistics are good enough and you perform well enough in college that professional scouts will either draft or sign you as a free agent?

A: No. Scouts don't care as much about your statistics as your potential; for example, this past season at Youngstown State, I caught for the number one draft pick of the San Francisco Giants, Brad Hennessey, who was a converted infielder just learning the intricacies of pitching and didn't have great stats as far as a win-loss record. But Brad threw the ball 93 miles an hour and had tremendous potential as a pitcher. The professional organizations know that if they have athletes with this much potential, they can teach them the game. There are many pitchers out there who know the game but will never be able to throw the ball that fast.

Author's note: *Todd is another example of an athlete never giving up on his dreams. Todd tried out for an independent professional team in the Northern League and made the team through his efforts to be seen and signed by a major league organization in the future.*

Todd teaches a young catcher the proper mechanics to block a baseball.

ADVICE FROM "COUNSELORS AND ADVISORS"

Advice from Wayne Bair, Guidance Counselor, Former Coach

Wayne has been a high-school guidance counselor for 25 years and junior-high guidance counselor for five years. Currently, he's at Brookfield High School in Ohio, a Division III school, with a senior class enrollment of 130.

Wayne's athletic background includes receiving a baseball scholarship at Division II Edinboro University in Pennsylvania where he was MVP of his team. He later was a high-school basketball and track coach and currently is a tennis coach.

Q: **As a former coach and guidance counselor who's advised numerous athletes for all NCAA division levels, what do you feel is the role of the guidance counselor in the athletic recruiting process?**

A: We've had students earn athletic scholarships to such schools as Ohio State, Michigan, Arizona, Penn State, Ohio University, Notre Dame, West Virginia, Miami, and other Division I schools. We've had many more students attend Division II and III schools. Three All-American athletes came from our small school, one of which, Marcus Marek, was recently inducted into the Ohio State athletic Hall of Fame.

Our coaches and I probably provide more assistance to the marginal athlete than anyone else. We honestly assess academic and athletic ability by using computer databases, helping us help students decide which schools are a good fit for them.

Q: **What advice do you have for high-school athletes with aspirations of participating in sports on the collegiate level?**

A: Academically, students must look at GPAs and ACT scores to determine if they can compete academically. Athletically, coaches must be honest in their assessments of what division levels athletes can play in. As a former college athlete, I recommend that the athletes err on the side of going where they are very likely to play.

Q: What advice do you have for parents or guardians of student athletes aspiring to participate in collegiate sports?

A: Parents need to be supportive of their kids' desire to continue their sport at the next level. Parents also must balance their child's time and energy so that their grades aren't compromised. *Don't take away their dream, but prepare them for the reality that competitive sports may just supplement one's college experience.*

Q: What advice do you have for student athletes concerning the transition from the high school to the collegiate sports level, both as a student and as an athlete?

A: College sports are structured differently from high-school sports. Athletes need to be intrinsically motivated. One reason athletes don't continue in college is that their large support system is no longer with them. Again, I recommend to go to a college where you can play and have fun.

Q: Do you feel that student athletes increase their chances of becoming athletically recruited if they have grades that are good enough to qualify for academic scholarships?

A: Yes. Division II and III can help some student athletes with only academic aid. Therefore, the students must make themselves more attractive if they can qualify for academic help.

Q: What advice do you have for student athletes and parents/guardians concerning where to find out and apply for possible academic scholarships?

A: At our school, I put out a list of scholarships, websites for financial aids, and orientation to OCIS software (Occupational Career Information Systems), which high schools use to help students find the specific information they seek concerning college programs. OCIS may be free to the public as soon as this fall. If OCIS is not available in your particular state, ask your guidance counselor about similar programs, such as COIN.

Q: What changes have arisen in the athletic recruiting process during the 25 years you've been a guidance counselor?

A: Now Division I coaches will *not* take a risk on athletes unless they're phenomenal athletes like Bo Jackson. Very few nonqualifier or partial qualifier student athletes are given scholarships.

Q: What's the difference among Division I, II, and III and junior colleges athletically, academically, and financially?

A: For Division I, you must be an exceptional athlete and then certain schools have higher academic standards than others. For example Duke University has higher standards, and Cincinnati not as high. For Divisions II and III, you must be a decent athlete and a decent student who's able to pay some of your own costs.

Q: Are there any guides or websites for student athletes and parents/guardians to research colleges and the necessary information needed to decide which colleges to attend?

A: We use OCIS, a computer database for academics (excellent search tools; Peterson's, which provides many search tools for academics and athletics (paperbacks); the Internet for searching for information; and paperback books with majors listed.

Q: What year in high school should students, regardless of athletic ability, speak to their guidance counselor about plans?

A: Students must begin serious preparation in grade 9; the courses they take that year affect the final GPA as much as courses in their senior year. Many colleges give academic money based on GPA for the four years and ACT scores.

Q: What are core courses and advanced placement courses and what's their importance?

A: Core classes are English, math, history, science, foreign language, and computers. Colleges, as well as the NCAA, use core courses to determine eligibility.

Q: Do student athletes have less chance of getting an athletic scholarship because they come from a small high school?

A: No, not today; the college coaches of today are looking for athletes that nobody else knows about. With high-school coaches pushing their athletes and making college coaches aware, the athletes can come from a large or a small high school.

Q: Explain how the high-school coach and the guidance counselor work together to assist and advise student athletes during the recruiting process.

A: Primarily, the coach is in the front line in assisting the student to get an athletic scholarship. If more time and research of schools is necessary, I have access to databases to sort for size of school, sports offered, and division of play.

Q: Is there any difference in the recruiting process between male and female sports?

A: Yes. Some of the female sports are just becoming strong, and the coaches are very receptive to phone calls from high schools.

Q: What advice would you give to a guidance counselor who is new to the collegiate athletic recruiting process?

A: Use common sense, use your computer to sort, don't be afraid to call a college coach or define your athlete in writing so that the coach can determine whether a potential student athlete may benefit by attending a certain school.

Q: What information should a guidance counselor provide a prospective student athlete and his/her parents/guardian concerning the NCAA's eligibility requirements?

A: The *NCAA Guide for the College-Bound Student-Athlete* is a "must read" for the athlete who plans to play sports in college. Until recently, the NCAA supplied high-school guidance counselors with complimentary copies of the guide that contained all of the information a prospective college student athlete needed to know concerning initial eligibility requirements.

Now that the NCAA has upgraded its website, their guide can be found by visiting the NCAA Clearinghouse Home Page at www.ncaaclearinghouse.net. Reach the website from links on the NCAA's main website: www.ncaa.org. All of the information a student athlete needs to know and understand is on this website.

The key features the new Clearinghouse services include, in addition to obtaining the NCAA guide on line, are the Division I and II eligibility requirements, core course listings for high schools, frequently asked questions (FAQs), and links to the NCAA website.

Author's note: *High-school guidance counselors are very busy people with limited time constraints, and very often the work they do is unappreciated by parents because they don't realize the enormous work load a counselor is responsible for in order to help all of the students, not just the ones who play sports.*

If you do not have a computer, go to a library and access this website free of charge or phone the Clearinghouse at one of its toll-free numbers: 877/262-1492 (Customer Service line from 8:00-5:00 Central Time, Monday-Friday), 877/861-3003 (the 24-hour NCAA Clearinghouse Initial Eligibility Hotline), or 888/388-9748 (NCAA Publication Division for a free copy of the guide mailed free). Getting the NCAA guide, which has the Student Release Form inside, is the first step a student athlete must take to be eligible to participate in college sports. The customer service line and hotline may come into play after the SRF has been returned to the Clearinghouse.

Coach Bair and the members of his 1995 record-setting 1600-meter relay girls' high-school track team.

Advice from Dave Smercansky, High-school Athletic Director, NCAA ERA Pitching Champion

Dave's background includes receiving a scholarship and pitching for Youngstown State University's Penguins and formerly coaching baseball at Boardman High School in Ohio, where he's currently the school's athletic director. He led the nation with an 0.36 ERA when he was a junior at Y. S. U. Even though Dave was a high-school baseball coach from Ohio, he has coached athletes who have received Division I athletic scholarships to colleges all across the country, such as Stanford University in California, University of North Carolina in Greensboro, University of Tampa in Florida, and Winthrop College in South Carolina.

Q: What do college coaches look for in athletes when they're recruiting?

A: The first and most important questions college coaches ask are about ACT and SAT scores and GPA; if the player is coachable; if he/she's a team player; what's his/her work ethic like; how many positions can the student athlete play at the collegiate level; and what kind of parents does the athlete have?

Q: What do you suggest that student athletes do to determine which division level is best suited for them to participate in?

A: They have to look at the role they want to fulfill. Do they want to play on a day-to-day basis, or do they want to be a role player?

Q: What do you feel are the most important factors for student athletes to be aware of in the transition from high school to a collegiate sports level?

A: Educational responsibilities and demands, as well as the level of competition and its demands.

Q: What should athletes do to get noticed and to promote themselves?

A: Go to camps and tryouts, and play in summer leagues. Be able to play multiple positions.

Q: What do college coaches look for besides size, speed, and strength when they recruit student athletes?

A: Coachability, grades (ACT and SAT), work ethic, demeanor, and pregame attitude.

Q: Do you have any advice for parents on the recruiting process?

A: Read the NCAA Clearinghouse manual; make sure students are carrying five credits. The manual lists all courses necessary and the sliding ACT/GPA mechanism. Find out if the university offers the program the athlete is pursuing.

Q: How important are communication skills as far as student athletes being able to clearly express themselves when talking to college recruiters?

A: Important—communication is an important factor—being able to articulate your concerns, wishes, etc.

Q: How important is a professional appearance when speaking to recruiters?

A: Extremely important to have a professional appearance. Colleges want you to represent their school with class; athletes are in the public eye.

Q: What advice do you have for junior-high athletes?

A: Play as many sports as possible; don't specialize in just one. And *grades, grades, grades*—develop your work habits.

Q: How do college coaches determine the amount of heart and desire a student athlete has?

A: Tough question, but I believe they evaluate very closely the way athletes deal with adversity. They also look to see how hard they are working at the game (practices, pregame, etc.).

Q: **What's your opinion on sports camps? Should students attend them?**

A: *Yes*! Great exposure.

Q: **Do you think you have to come from a big school to get an athletic scholarship?**

A: No. Coaches will find you. There are a lot of people who can provide coaches with information, such as alumni, umpires, etc.

Dave puts his degree in athletic administration to good use as the high-school athletic director.

Q: **Do you feel a student athlete's chances of being recruited increase if college coaches know the prospect may or will be receiving academic money for college?**

A: Yes, as far as Division II and III colleges go. This is all they can offer.

Q: **What are some of the negative factors that would immediately turn a college coach away from recruiting athletes, regardless of their talent?**

A: Attitude, individualism, and lack of coachability.

Advice from John Young, High-school Principal and Coach, Center for the University of Akron

John's background includes just about everything you can think of that is related to high-school sports and college scholarships. He was an All-City and All-Northeastern Ohio center for Cardinal Mooney High School in Youngstown, Ohio; he received a full football scholarship to the University of Akron. He earned a Masters in Administration from Youngstown State University. John coached high-school football and track and was a social studies teacher before becoming a high-school principal; He is the father of five children, two of whom were awarded college scholarships in athletics. His youngest son also will be a three-year letter winner at Cardinal Mooney High School. He is currently principal of Liberty High School located in Youngstown, Ohio.

Q: With all the experience you have accumulated over the years concerning the recruiting process that leads to athletic scholarships and/or financial aid, what advice do you have to offer student athletes and their parents?

A: As parents, we must expose and get our children involved in all areas from academics to athletics at an early age. My eldest son was playing community football in 6th-grade and my daughter was traveling around the state and the East Coast playing tournament softball at age 10. We didn't know if she had the talent, but her coaches worked hard and she was exposed to excellent competition. She was able to obtain a college scholarship. All of my children went to camps from big-time colleges to local community and high school camps. In their early high-school years, we sought out the best ACT/SAT tutors, and this helped greatly with college admissions. Be there for your kids; they really need you all the way through the process!

Q: What do you suggest that student athletes do to get noticed and recruited? Are attending sports camps a good idea?

A: As mentioned previously, go to as many camps as possible. If possible, volunteer to work or help at school or kiddie camps.

Many times, there are coaches who work with athletes in specific areas, such as pitchers or catchers during the off season. Seek out the best ; usually other parents know who is the best instructor. Don't be afraid to ask questions. Others like to talk about their children and their experiences, both good and bad. If you're a catcher or a receiver, volunteer to catch for the pitcher or the quarterback. It will definitely get you noticed; it happened with my child.

Q: **Concerning girls' sports specifically, what advice do you have to offer them concerning women's athletic scholarships?**

A: I never thought my little dancing daughter would be getting down and dirty as a collegiate softball catcher, but it happened. After seeing the college competition in girls' sports, if your daughter wants to play or enjoy sports like softball, basketball, soccer, and track, she *can* do it. There is money out there for female athletes. As a principal, I've seen many girls make it in both college athletics and academics.

Q: **Do you need to know someone, be lucky, or get a break to get an athletic scholarship?**

A: Any of these would certainly help, but everyone has to work to make it happen. The parents are the most important part. Get involved, encourage, and be there. Don't be abrasive but talk to friends, neighbors, other athletes, parents, and coaches and help your child set his/her *goals*. Have more than one goal in case another doesn't work out.

Q: **What do you feel are the most important factors for student athletes to be aware of in the transition from high school to a collegiate sports level?**

A: For myself, it becomes a year round endeavor even more in college. Most athletes come back and tell me how difficult it is in college especially in keeping up with academics. If you're not committed to studying and your classes, *don't* even attempt college athletics. The rewards are great especially with all the true friends you make. Your four or five years of college athletics fly by. You have to be committed to being the *best* both in athletics, as well as academics.

Advice from Jeffery Tarver, President of the Mentoring Student Athletes Foundation

Jeffery's background includes being a three-sport star at Brookfield High School in Brookfield, Ohio. He excelled in football as a defensive back, in basketball as a guard, and in track as a 440- relay man. He was a free safety for The Ohio State University football team for two years before sustaining a career-ending knee injury.

He is currently the president of the Mentoring Student Athletes Foundation located in Gahanna, Ohio, just outside of Columbus. The MSA Foundation is a non profit organization that helps minority students in grades 8-12. Each student is required to maintain a 2.5 grade point average. The MSA Foundation helps student athletes learn how to do self-evaluations so that they can learn how to sell themselves as attractive recruits in order to increase their chances of obtaining post secondary education or training (i.e., college, trade school, military, and vocational).

Q: Could you explain what the Mentoring Student Athletes Foundation does and how it is beneficial to junior-high and high–school athletes?

A: The Mentoring Student Athletes Foundation assists students in achieving their maximum potential in academic and social development by providing the essential resources for success. It is the MSA Foundation's belief that each student must possess strong academic and social skills to be prepared for post secondary education and training.

Q: What services are provided by the MSA Foundation?

A: We provide the following services: academic and personal advising sessions; study skills and test-taking strategy workshops; field trips to colleges and universities, recreational activities, and cultural centers; post-secondary and career workshops; and tutorial programs.

Q: What do you suggest high-school student-athletes do to promote themselves to college recruiters?

A: Academics! High-school student athletes need to promote themselves first and foremost by academics. Their athletic ability is secondary. Attending sports camps is an excellent way for high school athletes to showcase their talents. Sports camps are also a good setting for high-school athletes to see how they measure up to their competition. Young athletes need to attend as many camps as possible in order for them to realistically be able to evaluate their own talents so that they can get a better feel for the division level of athletic competition that is best suited for them.

My goal is to not only help these boys and girls learn how to promote themselves as attractive athletic recruits to colleges but also to help them learn how to promote themselves as attractive well-rounded academic recruits. My dream is that I want these youngsters to succeed in college and to understand that at some point in time in their future, they will not only have a chance to make a positive contribution to society, but they will also have the chance to cheerfully give something back to the communities that they grew up in.

Tarver with Ohio State alumni; Butch Reynolds (L), former World Class record holder in the 400 meters; and Joey Galloway (R), Dallas Cowboys' wide receiver at the Buckeye Celebrity Basketball Classic that was organized by Jeffery to raise funds for his Mentoring Student Athletes Foundation program, located in Columbus, Ohio.

Authors Note: *Jeffery, a fellow classmate of mine, is yet another fine example of an athlete giving something back to the game for the benefit of today's student-athletes. If you would like to know more about the Mentoring Student Athletes Foundation you can contact Jeffery at 1-800-608-1819 or by email at msaprogram@hotmail.com*

ADVICE FROM "PARENTS WITH EXPERIENCE"

Advice from Robert "Tut" Marek, Father of OSU Hall of Fame Son

"Tut" is a former athlete who participated in many sports and the father of Marcus Marek, a former All-American linebacker for the Ohio State Buckeyes. Marcus was recently inducted into the Ohio State Athletic Hall of Fame and is still the career tackling record holder for OSU. Tut's son was also an All-Ohio linebacker while playing for Brookfield High School, which won the state championship that year. Marcus later went on to play professional football for three years in the USFL for the Portland, New Orleans, and Boston Breakers and then briefly for the Cleveland Browns and Chicago Bears before suffering a career-ending injury.

Q: Could you describe what the collegiate athletic recruiting process was like for you and your son?

A: The recruiting process was one of the most exciting and memorable times of our lives, as well as for the rest of the family, the coaches, and friends. The opportunity of speaking to and meeting with college coaches from all across the country was an incredible experience.

At first, it was a pleasure for my son and me to receive all of the attention. Then the hard part came, which was deciding on which five colleges to visit. To make a long story short, before deciding on which colleges to visit, the most instrumental point of the entire process was when the legendary Woody Hayes came to the house for a visit and convinced the family that he wanted to make sure we understood why he was there personally: He intensely thought the best football players from Ohio should be playing only for the Buckeyes, which had a very proud and nationally recognized team.

Shortly after the visit from Hayes, the coach stepped down from head coaching ranks at OSU, and there was a time when the Buckeyes didn't have a coach. Mr. Hayes inspired my son, who was a very inspirational player himself, so much so that he'd already decided to attend Ohio State because of the program, the tradition, and the fact that he was proud not only to be recruited by Ohio State but also to become an Ohio State Buckeye.

Earl Bruce, who would become the new head coach, came to visit, as did Glen Mason, the offensive coordinator at the time and current head coach at the University of Minnesota. These coaches were just an extension of the proud tradition of Ohio State, and at that time, there never was any reason for concern from the standpoint of whether Ohio State would select the right coach and his staff for the opening for the new head coaching job. To no one's surprise, Bruce and his staff picked up right where Woody Hayes had left off.

Photo by Marc Jablonski

Left to right: Glen Mason, former Ohio State defensive coach and current University of Minnesota head football coach; Marcus Marek; Denny Fryzel, Ohio State defensive coach; and Robert Marek at an Ohio State University football awards banquet in Columbus, Ohio.

I was always there to support and advise my son during the decision-making process, but this was a decision that I strongly felt that my son had to make himself.

The recruiting process was not all a glamorous and exciting adventure, although there never was a dull moment; there were many headaches along the way. Once my son decided in his mind that he wanted to attend Ohio State—even before meeting Earl Bruce and his staff—there had to be a waiting period until that time officially came. During that time, even though all the other colleges knew my son intended to go to OSU, they still acted like vultures, knowing that this would be their last chance of ever talking an Ohio ball player out of attending Ohio State.

This became an irritating point in time and one in which I had to become more of a protector for my son rather than a father. There were actual incidents where I had to politely ask coaches to leave the property when they appeared with no warning that they were coming to visit. Many colleges would not take "no" for an answer; I hope that it was only because that Ohio State didn't officially have a coach at that time.

Q: Do you have any advice for high-school student athletes on the collegiate recruiting process?

A: First of all, keep in the back of your mind that you're going to college to get an education that you'll be using towards your future in the time period starting in four to five years from when you first attend college and then for the rest of your life. Hopefully, some day you'll become a pro athlete, but you can't put all of your eggs in one basket. What if you get injured or you're just not good enough to make it to the next level? Then what are you going to do? Don't be afraid to ask the college coaches questions, such as "What position do you plan on using me? Who is playing at those positions now? Why do you think your college program is better for me than somebody else's?"

Mr. Marek (R), and his son Marcus, enjoy time together after an Ohio State football awards banquet in Columbus, Ohio.

Q: Do you have any advice for parents during the collegiate athletic recruiting process?

A: Support your child as much as possible and let him/her make the final decision on which college to attend. Make sure you discuss with him/her all of the factors that you, as a parent, feel worth mentioning: athletics, academics, the location of the school, and the distance from home. Don't be afraid to ask college coaches questions about their philosophy, the length of their contract as a coach, or what position they see your child playing on the team.

Ask your child to explain to you why he/she's deciding on a certain school. If you feel the answers aren't for the right reasons, don't be afraid to say so. Even though the final decision will ultimately be his/hers, as a parent, you must make sure that in his/her mind, the child knows he/she's choosing a certain school for the right reasons.

Robert Marek (R) and his son, Marcus, holding a rose signifying Ohio State's victory that led to a game in the Rose Bowl in Pasadena, California.

Photo by Marc Jablonski

Advice from Milan Zordich, Father of an All-American

Milan is a former athlete from Youngstown, Ohio, who participated in several sports and is the father of Michael Zordich, a former All-American defensive back at Penn State University. Michael was heavily recruited by many major college programs and went on to become a professional defensive back for the New York Jets, St. Louis and Arizona Cardinals, and the Philadelphia Eagles.

Q: **Do you have any advice for junior-high and high-school student athletes?**

A: Follow your dreams and *hit the books*!

Q: **Do you have any advice for parents on the athletic recruiting process?**

A. Keep an eye on your children and make sure they're doing the right things academically, athletically and socially, and staying out of trouble.

Q: **Do you have any advice for student athletes and parents/ guardians when it comes time to make their final decision on what college to select to continue their athletic career?**

A: I feel that the parents and student athletes should discuss all of the options together and that the student athlete should make the final decision. Sometimes that decision can be very difficult, and you may have to make the decision based on which head coach you like the most. You may have to go on a gut feeling and the background of the coach who's recruiting you if other factors like the athletic and academic programs are all equal.

Milan's son, Michael, raises the intensity level of his fellow teammates on the Philadelphia Eagles sidelines.

Advice from Andy Timko Sr., Father of an Oriole

Andy Sr. is a former stand-out athlete and coach from Youngstown, Ohio. His two sons were great athletes: Bruce, who attended Youngstown State University on a basketball scholarship, and Andy, who gave the interview just before this one—a 3rd-round draft pick by the Baltimore Orioles right out of high school.

Dad Timko was faced with a tough situation then: How to advise his son Andy Jr., who'd received a baseball scholarship and signed a Letter of Intent to Alabama University and then was drafted in the 3rd round as a shortstop for the Orioles?

As a parent, he wanted to give the best advice possible, and since he's never experienced a similar situation, he knew he needed experienced counsel. He contacted Frank Dravecky, father of Dave Dravecky, a pitcher for the Pittsburgh Pirates' organization at that time. (Later, Dave went on to a major league career with the San Francisco Giants and the San Diego Padres before sustaining a career-ending injury.)

The Timkos and Draveckys lived in the same area, and Andy Sr. asked Frank's advice about Andy Jr.'s choices: turning pro right out of high school or going on to college on a baseball scholarship to one of the best baseball programs in the country.

Frank Dravecky's advice was that no matter what route they chose, Andy Jr. must get an education at some point. "Are the Baltimore Orioles offering your son enough money to pay for his education?" Frank asked. "Playing in the minor leagues is very difficult, especially for an athlete right out of high school. What if he gets hurt or never makes it to the major leagues? What would he have to fall back on?"

The Timko males negotiated a contract with the Orioles where the organization would pay Andy Jr. enough so that they could bank some of the money for college. Later on, the shortstop graduated from Youngstown State University with a degree in business.

Andy Sr.'s advice to high-school student athletes and their parents who find themselves in a similar situation: Seek counsel from somebody who's been there and find contacts who can give insight and answer questions. "Don't be afraid to ask questions," Andy Sr., says. "Answers to situations like this aren't going to come to you. Obviously, you'll have each party involved trying to persuade you [to play for their team]. You *absolutely* need to find counsel who is impartial to each party to help you make your decision."

Three generations of Andy Timkos: Andy R. Timko with his grandson, Andy E. Timko (C) and his son, Andy B. Timko, after his grandson's summer league baseball game.

Advice from Ray Bowers, Father of NCAA Career Leading Rusher, R. J. Bowers

Ray Bowers is the father of R. J. Bowers, the all-time leading rusher in the history of NCAA football. R. J. just broke the rushing record this past season as a halfback for Grove City College, Grove City, Pennsylvania.

R. J. was drafted in the 11th round by the Houston Astros out of West Middlesex (PA) High School and played five years in the minor league system as an outfielder. Then he suffered a baseball career-ending wrist injury. Fortunately, when he'd signed his baseball contract, the Astros agreed to pay for his college education, and he chose Grove City. Currently, R. J. is playing for the Cleveland Browns after playing the previous season for the Pittsburgh Steelers.

Ray is also the father of two other athletes: Steve, who attended West Virginia on a baseball scholarship at the Division III level, and his youngest son, Bill, who attended Hiram College in Ohio, where he was awarded institutional funding—basically another name for an athletic scholarship at Division III level.

Ray didn't participate in athletics in high school or college because he had to go work at any early age. He worked in the maintenance department of North Star Steel in Youngstown for close to 20 years and wanted to give his sons the things he wasn't able to do when he was growing up.

Q: Do you have any advice for high-school student athletes who may have the opportunity to choose between signing a professional contract or accepting an athletic scholarship to attend college?

A: *The bottom line is you need an education,* but if you decide to go pro, have your scholarship money put aside by putting it into your contract before you sign. We negotiated this for R. J. In the case of my son Steve, who was watched by several scouts in high school, the scouts contacted me about drafting him for their professional organizations but said that he'd probably be selected in a lower round. This meant that he'd get less money and not enough for a college education. My answer to those scouts was not to select him for the draft if they couldn't guarantee enough money for college because he was quite happy with his West Virginia baseball scholarship offer. I also said that they could continue to follow him in his college career if they were still interested.

Q: Do you have any advice for parents concerning the previous question?

A: You must be there for them to discuss all possibilities involved with such a serious decision. Don't force any decision because it must be their own. Once again, the bottom line is: *They need an education!* If the professional contract offered isn't large enough to provide for a college education, seriously consider taking the sure thing with the scholarship rather than gambling on your son making it to the big leagues. The odds are very slim for any ball player making it to the major leagues, and that's where the money is—not in the minors.

Q: What advice do you have for high-school student athletes when it comes to selecting a college to attend?

A: Before you visit colleges, investigate and research those you are interested in, not just for their athletic recruiting needs and traditions but also for their academic programs. When you visit, determine if that college is the place you'll be comfortable living at for the next four years. Find out about extracurricular activities on campus or nearby.

My son Steve fell in love with West Virginia University and the surrounding area outside the campus in Morgantown. He loves the outdoors and liked the fact that he could hunt and fish in his free time. That was the deciding factor in choosing WVU even though he had scholarship offers from other schools.

Advice from Don Watt, Coach, Father of a 2001 Scholarship Recipient

Don's background includes experience as a former athlete who's coached baseball for 15 years, currently for the Astro Falcon Baseball Organization in Struthers, Ohio. His son was a 2001 high school graduate and received a baseball scholarship at Akron University, Akron, Ohio.

Don is involved with Rip's Sports Lounge, a family-owned and operated restaurant that's frequented by college coaches of all sports, as well as baseball scouts during baseball season. He's sharing advice he's gathered over the years from coaches and scouts: Be aware, he says, that many coaches and scouts appear an hour or so before the actual game time to watch the behavior and practice habits of the prospect they're scouting.

They want to see if the prospect shows up early or just on time for the game, along with how he prepares himself for the game. Is he playing pepper? Is he hitting in the cages? Is he dressed properly?

Don says that once a prospect's name is listed in one scout's book, he'll be listed in all of them, and, therefore, the college coaches also will be aware of the prospect. The key is to keep your name in that book, Don says. Don't have your name crossed out because you do something stupid before the game even starts.

While the game is in progress, scouts and recruiters evaluate the prospect's behavior, such as not hustling on the field or lack of composure after an unsuccessful event at the plate or in the field. They notice whether the prospect throws his helmet or bat in anger or hangs his head and looks depressed after failing. These actions will immediately get his name crossed off the list.

Coaches and scouts have hundreds of potential prospects they're watching each year. Appearing at games is their way of eliminating the prospects who aren't worth investing in for one reason or another.

Don's son must have followed his dad's advice, along with being a good athlete, because he was fortunate enough to have a choice of several colleges. "Help your child as much as possible in his/her decision of which college to attend, but allow him/her to make the final decision about which college and coach he/she will feel most comfortable with for the next four years of his/her life," Don advises.

Q: Do you feel that there is an exact step-by-step process that a high-school athlete can follow to guarantee an athletic scholarship?

A: No, every recruiting situation is different. It's up to the athlete to perform well in the classroom and on the field whenever you play in front of a college recruiter.

The best advice I can give as a parent of an athlete who just received a Division I athletic scholarship is for the athlete to work hard at his/her game and grades and get him/herself seen by as many college coaches as possible, whether it's in a game, at a college camp, a recruiting showcase, etc.

More advice: A parent should help the child by also visiting the colleges that are interested. Parents should realistically take into account and discuss the current and upcoming team rosters of the colleges to find out if there are already several players at the same position that their child plays.

Coach Watt at the Sports Bar and Resaurant he owns and operates called Rip's Sports Cafe in Struthers, Ohio.

PROMOTE

YOURSELF

College Coaches Offer Advice on Promoting Yourself

In a recent one-on-one survey, many college coaches and scouts at a high-school Connie Mack baseball tournament were asked questions about the recruiting process. Regardless of the sport involved, the same questions apply to coaches and scouts.

Q: In what grade do you start tracking recruits?

A: It depends on the coach or scout. Some follow prospects from their freshman year and watch them mature; some spot them at camps in junior high. All coaches said that athletes need to be noticed by their junior year to increase chances of getting scholarships. Although it's not impossible for a senior to have a great season in his/her sport and get an athletic scholarship, the odds are against it because coaches and scouts haven't followed his/her progress very long. Coaches also check out academic backgrounds and character references.

Q: What percentage of student athletes have you ever recruited without seeing them play?

A: The answer was unanimous among coaches: Zero! Coaches don't offer scholarships without watching athletes perform. This can be at tryout camps, showcases, or high-school or college sports camps, as well as games. They don't rely on videos, statistics, or accomplishments sent by parents, coaches, or recruiting services.

After speaking to hundreds of coaches across the country, we heard of only twice where a scholarship was offered without the coach seeing the prospect perform: 1. Andy Timko, who was recommended to the Alabama coach by a prominent senior scout, and 2. a student athlete from a well-respected California junior college team that had yielded several previous athletes, who was recommended by a well-respected coach of that school, along with coaches of every team in that conference. That unnamed student received a partial scholarship because of an urgent need to fill the position—one scholarship athlete had signed a professional contract, and another was transferring to another school.

Q: How many recruits do you evaluate each year?

A: Thousands! Every sport is basically the same when it comes to how many prospects are evaluated each year. A college baseball coach will evaluate two teams of nine players each in a game; that coach and his staff will watch well over 100 games a season. A college football coach will evaluate two teams of a minimum of 11 players each because not everyone plays both offense and defense.

(College football recruiting is a major corporation versus recruiting for smaller sports because of the amount of money generated—which ultimately supports other sports programs.)

Q: How many letters do you receive daily or yearly?

A: Some coaches said that they get at least 10 letters daily; others say well over 40, depending on the sport, the division level, and the program's tradition. Do coaches read all of the letters they receive? Yes, say the coaches, unless they're from a recruiting service; those usually get pitched out. How much of each letter does the coach read? It depends on the professionalism of the letter and the background of the writer (coach, alumnus, friend, etc.). Letters with only statistics about the player aren't taken seriously.

Q: Do you prefer to recruit in-state or out-of-state?

A: It depends on the type of sport involved. Most major college football and basketball programs can afford to recruit out-of-state. Coaches of nonrevenue sports said they'd prefer to recruit in-state in most circumstances if players are available. For example, the state of West Virginia had only nine players receive Division I scholarships for baseball. Some smaller states don't have enough potential recruits or qualified players in their state. The more successful a college sports program, the more likely they are to recruit out-of-state.

Also, many colleges don't have enough money in their budgets to recruit out-of-state. When narrowing your choices of colleges to visit, ask the coach questions about size, availability of potential in-state recruits, etc.

One coach said that you can save yourself as much as $2,000 on your out-of-state tuition if you live in certain counties within a certain radius of a campus in a nearby state, called a Regional Service Area.

Q: Do you feel that recruiting services are necessary or valuable tools for athletes promoting themselves?

A: The majority of college coaches don't have kind words for recruiting services! Many coaches said that letters from recruiting services are pitched into the wastebasket immediately! Money spent on those services, coaches said, could be better used by the parents for the child's education.

Travel time and cost and definite out-of-state tuition prevent coaches from seeing prospects who live hundreds or thousands of miles away. A video of an athlete practicing or performing in a game situation can be very helpful, they said, but a video alone won't get anyone an athletic scholarship. But, they said, a video can be taken seriously if it's done by an individual who knows what a college coach is looking for.

Be sure that all information on the video is accurate! One coach watched a baseball player's video, showing him running 60 yards, and the stopwatch in the corner of the video said that he ran it in 6.8 seconds. The coach got out his own stopwatch and timed the run— 8.0 seconds! Ooops! Recruiting services who try to bamboozle coaches end up losing credibility, and the parents' money spent for promotion gets wasted.

Q: How should athletes determine which division level is best suited for them?

A: Coaches said that the division level is usually dictated by the letters and phone calls the student athlete gets after July 1 going into the senior year. Don't think that questionnaires mean much; colleges send out thousands of them.

The coaches said many 17- and 18-year-olds can't realistically compare and evaluate themselves to other athletes. It's practically impossible for athletes and their parents to be realistic, the coaches said. They noted that student athletes should be more realistic after they've digested all of the information we're presenting in this guide. "Isn't that the main reason you're writing this guide?" several coaches asked.

Q: How many walk-ons do you add to your team yearly?

A: It depends on the number of roster spots available each year in each sport, as well as the program's needs. Contact the college coach before trying out for the team because he/she might not be in the market for your position, regardless of how good you may be. All coaches polled have 20 percent or fewer walk-ons on their teams. Remember that only a few make the team out of the 100 or so trying out.

Q: How many junior-college transfers do you add to your team yearly?

A: This, too, depends on the needs of the sports teams' rosters and positions. Junior-college transfers are beneficial because of college experience and maturity, but they have only two or three years to play. One coach had as much as 30 percent of his roster from junior colleges, two to three times higher than average as a whole for college sports programs. Junior-college transfers are on the rise, however.

Q: Should a prospect send you a video of him/herself?

A: Yes, said coaches. Just make sure it's not time-consuming—no more than three to five minutes, showing correct angles and situations involved with the athlete's sport.

Q: Do you watch internet videos?

A: No, the coaches said, although they said it's a good idea, but they don't have the time to wait for the videos to download. Besides, they said, some are so distorted that they can't effectively evaluate the athletes. Until this technology is improved, it's not a valuable tool.

Q: What are the parents' roles (NCAA rules, researching/visiting colleges, grades/attitude)?

A: To take charge of all of these, said the coaches, know the eligibility requirements, be sure that the athletes are registered with the NCAA Clearinghouse, and send in the FAFSA and scholarship forms as soon as possible. Let the athletes themselves speak to the coaches as much as possible; parents can find out more when they visit the school. Hammer on the importance of good grades, beginning in 9th grade, to ensure that the athletes are in control of their own destiny and working toward money for a college education, which may have to come from academic scholarships rather than athletic scholarships.

Q: What do you want to know about the parents' background?

A: To discover if they have any athletic background (coaching, participation, etc.) or if any of their other children were involved in collegiate sports. Some coaches are also interested in the height/weight of various family members. Mostly, they want to know if the FAFSA forms are correct because income determines the amount of financial aid.

Q: How are attending college sports camps helpful (exposure, instructional advice, comparing skills for determining level of play)?

A: Extremely important, coaches said. They can't always come to you, so why not go to them so they can see your skills, strength, speed, and attitude. There's no better way than camps, coaches said, because you'll not only be noticed, but you'll also pick up tips to improve your skills and learn how to evaluate and compare your own abilities. Student athletes: call the coach yourself to ask if he/she thinks you should attend his/her camp.

Q: Does the prospect's chances of being recruited increase if the coach knows he/she will be receiving financial aid because of his/her academics?

A: Unanimous answer: Yes! Coaches want eligible players, the best they can find, and aren't going to take a chance on a great athlete if his grades aren't satisfactory. Coaches must answer to their superiors regarding recruits who want "student" to come before "athlete." Some colleges require recruits to have at least a 3.0 GPA. Financial aid for athletes is especially important in Division II and III, as well as nonrevenue sports.

Q: Who are the most credible references? (high-school coach, opposing coach, alumni, personal trainer, teachers, employers)

A: A well-respected high-school coach is the best reference a player can have, especially if he/she puts in a good word for a player on another team. In baseball, a pro scout is the best reference. Opposing athletes' recommendations carry lots of weight; current or former collegiate or pro athletes and coaches are good references, as well as alumni who contact the coach with recommendations based on the athletes' abilities.

Personal trainers aren't always good references because they're being paid by you and will recommend you for that reason. He/she's not going to charge you for services and then not put in a good word; that, in essence, would be biting the hand that feeds him/her. Teachers and employers also tend to be partial to student athletes.

Recruiting Services
—the Good, the Bad, and the Ugly

This can be a very controversial chapter—depending on the viewpoint of the individual reader. Coaches will probably love it because we tell the truth about some of the areas that bug them. Parents will be glad to find out the ins and outs that can save them lots of money. And recruiting services themselves will probably not be happy to have someone blow the whistle on some of their ideas and business practices.

Actually, the recruiting service concept isn't all bad. It's just that everybody doesn't need to contract with an agency when, with a little hard work, you can achieve comparable results without going broke in the process. The big problems with a recruiting service lie in the fact that it's a business run by business people rather than people with athletic backgrounds, and it's very expensive!

So we advise you to read this chapter with an open mind and then make your own decision, based on your own circumstances, as to whether you want to sign up with a recruiting service or do it yourself, probably with equivalent or even better results.

GOOD

The more times a college coach hears an athlete's name, the better. A respectable recruiting service can help a student athlete get an athletic scholarship if it has a credible person acting as the scout, promoter, or advisor. A professionally filmed video, filmed from angles that a coach wants to see, is the best substitute for a coach seeing a player's skill without seeing him/her perform in person.

Services can provide coaches with the true height and weight of an athlete. (Can't you do that?)

ovide confirmed running times, vertical jumps, and various lifting results by credible reference people. Believe it or hool coach isn't always considered your most credible nding on the particular high-school coach's background. e coaches are aware that each high-school coach will favor r athlete over another almost any day of the week, where a service tends to be less partial. This isn't bad—it's just the truth.

It never hurts and can only help if you have another person involved besides your coach to list your accomplishments. This person can be a personal instructor or opposing coach who can be an excellent character reference. Be sure to have that person write a paragraph or so for you concerning your abilities, work ethics, and character. There is no better reference than an opposing coach because he/she has little to gain by helping you.

Suggestions: Check out where athletes from your county, league, or region are being recruited and which recruiting services and scouts, if any, are assisting them. Ask other athletes or parents if they have used a recruiting service and what they thought of it: Did it help? Was it worth the money? Would it be a good service for you or your student athlete?

Get on the internet and find "recruiting services internet player profiles for athletes" in your state or region to see how they compare to you and if they have gone to college on an athletic scholarship. Ask the scout or representative of that service which area players he/she says he/she has helped. See if he/she mentions all of them in your area or just the ones he/she helped out.

BAD

Some recruiting services charge an enormous amount of money. *Don't be fooled* when many recruiting services say that they have a 90 percent success rate for getting athletes scholarships. They also include, as part of their success rate, the fact that these student athletes may receive an academic scholarship from a university. Keep in mind that many of these services deal only with athletes who are already getting questionnaires from college coaches and have a 3.0 GPA.

Some services make fancy videos of players, with considerable emphasis on flare and little regard to content. For example, music in the background seems like a nice touch, but it does absolutely nothing to help get you recruited. Coaches are inundated with thousands of game tapes every year. They aren't interested in music or other needless embellishments because they just don't have the time. In order for a potential recruit to get the consideration he/she deserves, there must be the necessary clear, concise video footage and accurate personal, academic, and athletic information. Anything that helps a coach in making this task easier reflects well on the athlete.

While internet videos appear to be a fantastic idea, they're not as helpful as they appear, especially since recruiters really don't have time to spare for the internet, as you've been led to believe. Very few coaches will take the time to watch videos supplied to them through the internet because of download time. This often takes several valuable minutes before the coach can actually see the player's performance, and often the image is small, slow, and/or distorted.

Even in this computer age, most college coaches aren't familiar with the internet. In many cases, anything connected with internet recruiting is delegated to a younger coach or graduate-assistant coach in his/her early 20's who is more comfortable with computers. And regardless of the younger person's athletic ability, he/she is seriously lacking in knowledge and experience in recruiting expertise compared with the head coach or his/her paid assistants.

UGLY

Are you ready for this? Professional recruiting services can charge as much as $2,500 to promote a student athlete with no guarantees that the coaches they are contacting for you will even view the information sent to them—nor can they guarantee a scholarship. They may not even supply you with any documentation or confirmation that they have even sent out promotional packages in the first place.

Some recruiting services, to ensure their credibility with coaches, will deal only with student athletes who are already receiving questionnaires and have a 3.0 or above GPA.

These services also have many people working for their company simply because they had enough money to buy franchises in the area you live in. Many times, these so-called "scouts" never received an athletic scholarship themselves or never did any coaching on high-school or collegiate levels themselves. These people are simply salesmen—not qualified advisors for you to risk paying as much as $2,500 to promote your child.

Fortunately, not all recruiting services work this way. Please be sure to check the credentials of the scout who contacts you. Ask who he/she has helped to get an athletic scholarship—not financial aid, which you can get yourself by filling out the applications at the right time. One exception is a Division III program, where an athlete can't get an athletic scholarship but can get institutional funding from the school for participating in athletics.

Remember that for the most part, Division III schools cost much more money to attend than Division I and II schools, and although a recruiting service may say it helped a student athlete get $8,000 to go to college, they aren't telling you that the family must pay the balance of $12,000. This computes to a $20,000-a-year Division III school, and you could go to a $12,000-a-year higher division school without any assistance.

Other "Services" from the Services

Recruiting publications: These are put out by the recruiting services that rate top players of various sports. Some publications are much more respectable than others. You may look at one of their lists of top players, not see somebody who's well-deserving, and wonder why he/she isn't included in the list. For example, how could an athlete who was an All-State performer for two years in his/her sophomore and junior years not be listed in the top 100 players in the state? Often it's simply because the athlete didn't fill out and return the questionnaire from this publication. This isn't true for all recruiting publications, but the majority operate this way.

And very often, prospects who are listed are from larger high schools who receive more media exposure. The more successful a prospect's team is and the more it progresses through tournament action, the more exposure he/she gets.

College scouting services: These are impartial services paid for by various colleges to evaluate high-school prospects. They aren't affiliated with any particular college and basically observe the talent, skills, attitude, and character of the prospects for the coaches. They don't recruit players; they simply submit their opinions and information to college coaches.

The college coaches seriously evaluate the information sent to them from these types of services because these services aren't in the business of promoting these athletes. These services work for the college coaches, not the parents or student athletes.

Mailings and faxes by recruiting services: Usually mailing directly to a coach is the best way to assure that you'll have your promotional information read. Most college coaches are strongly advised to open their mail and read it because they never know if the person writing was told to do so by the coach's superior within the college, i. e., the school's president, the athletic director, or a well-respected alumnus or friend.

Many college coaches will tell you that ideally they want the prospect's information sent on the letterhead of their high-school or summer-league coach. A name recognized by the coach is next on the list, and then a letter from the student athlete. A letter from a questionable recruiting service is way down on the coach's list; since different coaches favor different services, you're always taking a chance with the recruiting service you choose. You've no idea how much mail a college coach receives daily and how much is thrown away without ever being opened. Faxes suffer the same consequences as letters since many of the same principles apply.

Internet recruiting and scouting services (internet player profiles): Don't be fooled by internet recruiting services who say that college coaches come to their website to check out the internet player profiles of student athletes!

Many internet services out there will charge about $50 to post a player profile resume on their website and tell you that college coaches come to their website to look for potential recruits.

Very often, these companies are out of business in a year or so. You can't just place a profile with a student athlete's accomplishments and statistics on the website and expect a college coach to believe that all of the information is accurate and then call or come knocking at your door!

You're underestimating the coaches' intelligence if you do. You have to realize that coaches will know that any height, weight, speed, and other information, if not confirmed by a credible reference, will be greatly exaggerated by the athlete him/herself. *If* a coach would possibly come to a website, and they seldom do, he/she could tell in a minute whether that website was respectable or not.

What you need to do is to ask the service what proof they have that college coaches actually come to their website.

Do any coaches use the internet? Lower-division level colleges or Division I nonrevenue or small revenue-generating college sports coaches are most inclined to use the internet to locate a potential prospect. Their limited recruiting budgets don't allow them much for traveling expenses to scout a prospect personally as higher-division athletic budgets do. Upper-division athletic programs generate an enormous amount of money not only for their own sport but also for other athletic programs at their schools and don't use the internet.

Author's note: *I originally considered starting a recruiting service of my own to promote student athletes to college coaches. After talking to the many college coaches I personally know and hearing the horror stories of what college coaches really think of recruiting services as a whole, I quickly decided against doing so. Sure, I would have been a credible source to all of the coaches I personally know, but what about the ones I didn't know? It takes a credible recruiting service years to establish a good relationship with college coaches, and daily I would be fighting the fact that so many recruiting services ahead of me have supplied college coaches with questionable information and taken parents for a huge financial ride with nothing to show for it. I can't be a part of that. I don't want to say that most recruiting services scam people, but I will say that many definitely aren't realistically aware of what the college coaches consider credible and important information about athletes.*

I would like to take this moment to recommend a company that I have discovered to be very effective in the recruiting game. Founded by a former NFL player and college recruiting casualty, DVD recruiting is not a "recruiting service." Instead, DVD Recruiting is a leading provider of video recruiting tools for high-school athletes, helping them find college athletic scholarships and competitive opportunities. DVD Recruiting incorporates an athlete's game tapes and other relevant and required information on CD-rom and DVD format. They're organized with interactive menus and designed for recruiters to easily navigate through all of the information needed to evaluate someone as a potential recruit. To find out more about DVD recruiting, call (800) 919-0902 or visit their website at www.dvdrecruiting.com

Get Noticed at Camps

Learn the rules of your game. Find out how to run, hit, tackle, jump, catch, receive, spike, or whatever maneuvers your specific sport requires. Interact with other athletes and coaches in the sport you love most.

How? Go to camp in the summertime! Just about every sport offers summer camps that specialize in teaching young people about a particular athletic activity. It's a great way to promote yourself and get noticed while learning more about it. Your athletic director or your coach knows what camps are where and has brochures giving information about the locations, dates, times, costs, and activities of each camp that focuses on your favorite sport.

Gino Toretta (R), 1992 Heisman Trophy winner from the University of Miami, Florida, instructing high-school quarterback Ron Stoops (L) at a summer football camp.

Most camps are offered at colleges and universities that are on the lookout for promising athletes. Coaches and their staffs, often along with a professional athlete or two, are there to teach the fundamentals to young athletes. High school athletes go to camps for the instruction on specifics and to showcase their talents to the coaches.

This is a good opportunity for young athletes, especially because certain divisions often invite coaches and scouts from lesser divisions to participate as instructors.

The photos in this section were taken at only one summer sports camp called the Camp of Champions that was held for youngsters (grades 3-8) at the Cardinal Mooney High School Field in Youngstown, Ohio. It should give you a good idea of how much valuable information can be obtained from camp instructors when attending a sports camp. This camp cost only $45.00 to attend.

(L-R) Bob Stoops, head football coach of the University of Oklahoma 2000 national championship team; Mark Stoops, defensive backs coach of the University of Miami, Florida, 2001 national championship team; Mike Stoops, associate head coach of the University of Oklahoma 2000 national championship team; Bernie Kosar, former quarterback for the Cleveland Browns and the University of Miami, Florida; Ron Stoops, defensive coordinator for Cardinal Mooney H.S. in Youngstown, Ohio.

Mark "Bo" Pelini, defensive coordinator for the University of Nebraska with Marcus Yensick (L) and Joey Kirila (R).

Michael Zordich, Philadelphia Eagles, (Penn State All-American defensive back), autographs a football for camper.

How to Promote Yourself

Other than having scouts from all of the colleges flocking to your games to watch you play, the best way to be noticed and recruited is by sending a professional-looking profile to a college coach, along with a professional-looking video tape and a personal evaluation from a credible source.

This is the most professional and logical way to promote yourself correctly. This is also much less expensive and more effective than hiring a recruiting service to do it for you. When you're in charge of sending your own information, you can be 100 percent sure that it is actually being sent out. You can even follow up with a phone call to be sure that the college coach received your package.

Scott Knox, a current high-school baseball coach and president of the Line-Drive Baseball Academy, puts together video packages and evaluation profiles and offers good advice on how and what to put in a profile package. Scott was a baseball coach at Youngstown State University and played in the Pittsburgh Pirates' minor leagues for three years. His advice is worth taking.

Include in a professional baseball video package a video tape of the student athlete demonstrating his/her skills in various hitting and fielding positions. The athlete also should be timed in the distance that is usually referred to in that sport. For example, for baseball, it's the 60-yard dash. For football, it's the 40-yard dash. These videos are most effective if they are taken by a credible coach who's aware of what situations a college coach would like to see the prospect showcasing during a workout.

Besides the videotape, an evaluation for the profile should be made by the coach on the athlete's performance, skills, which college division level is best suited for the athlete academically, etc. This should all be included with the video and given to the athlete to send to the top colleges of his/her choice. Also included in this profile should be the student athlete's grades and his/her NCAA Clearinghouse registration pin number.

Once this is finalized, the student athlete and parents should sit down and discuss which colleges are best-suited for his/her athletic and academic abilities. Then you should send your promotional package to the coach of your sport at the colleges of your choice. Be realistic when choosing your colleges and seriously consider what the coach has suggested in his evaluation.

"I charge in the vicinity of $300 to coordinate the workout, film and edit the video, fill out the evaluation form, include a copy of this guide and one that contains information about contacting college coaches, and then return the entire package to the student athlete," Scott says. This is a much more affordable and credible way of marketing the student athlete to coaches than paying a recruiting service that doesn't handle the videotaping itself. They'll charge you for editing the video or having you edit it yourself and pay for that on top of their promotional fees, which range from $1,000 to $2,500. Many times, the recruiting scout or representative handling your promotional packaging and evaluation isn't a former college coach or athlete who received an athletic scholarship.

Scott says, "The way I handle helping student athletes to promote themselves is much more professionally and credibly done and unbelievably less expensive. You'll need to pay for your own mailings to the colleges of your choice, but this cost will be minor since you don't need to send a video package and profile evaluation to every college in the country. Doing it yourself is the *only* way that you can be 100 percent sure that your promotional information has actually been sent."

Remember that many colleges outside of your state will first look at your home state because they have to consider the cost of out-of-state tuition when dealing with limited scholarships in a low-budget program or nonrevenue sport like baseball.

Zack Walz, a former Arizona Cardinals linebacker and victim of the hardships of recruiting, offers athletes an innovative and effective approach to marketing themselves to colleges across the country. To find out more about his company, DVD Recruiting, go to page 182 in the Recruiting Services chapter or visit their website at www.dvdrecruiting.com.

Communicating with College Coaches

It's important for student athletes to make their own connections with coaches of colleges they want to attend rather that let parents do it. And it's not really as overwhelming as it appears.

Once you've done your initial homework—that is, contacting the schools themselves for information about the academics, financial aid, room and board, and all of the other "college" stuff—you need to write letters to the coaches of your sport, introducing yourself and requesting their program packet that gives lots of information about many facets of their athletic program, as well as an athletic questionnaire. Once you see what's involved and fill out the questionnaire, everything will start to fall in place.

We're listing topics that should be incorporated in your introductory letter, which, by the way, should be well written on a typewriter or computer with no errors in spelling, grammar, or punctuation. Think of it as a cover letter for a job, and present yourself in a brief, polite, informative, and intelligent manner. And remember that you can't write a form letter to send out to everyone.

DO

1. Introduce yourself by name, high school, and graduation date.

2. Say why you want to go to that particular school.

3. Give a brief background that includes academic accomplishments, GPA, field of study, and class rank.

4. Include long-term and short-term athletic and academic goals.

5. Ask for the college's program packet and questionnaire.

6. Conclude with telephone numbers where you can be reached.

7. Keep copies of letters that you send.

8. Have someone who writes well look the letters over before you send them.

DON'T

1. Fill the letter with statistics and trivial information.

2. Include a letter of recommendation at this time.

Author's note: *If you are looking for help finding updated information on how to find the addresses of all NCAA colleges and universities listed in the U.S. and, more important, the name of the current college coach you wish to send a letter or email to, then visit www.collegecoachesonline.com or call (303) 988-9140.*

Andy Gold, owner of College Coaches Online, a parent of a recent scholarship athlete who has experienced the difficulty of obtaining such information, has designed a CD to help save high school coaches, students, and their parents countless hours of time surfing the internet or flipping through pages of an outdated book for the names of the current college coaches at every division level in the country.

I personally recommend that you visit this website or call Andy himself if you intend to promote yourself to college coaches. College Coaches Online is not a recruiting service. They endorse the "do it yourself" approach to college selection and can save you countless hours researching colleges. This CD also helps student athletes to narrow their focus of schools by matching their academic and athletic abilities with the requirements of each college or university. The CD contains a database of over 10,000 current college coaches in NCAA Divisions I, II and III. You will be able to find coaches' names, address, and phone numbers in seconds. You also will be able to search for colleges by specific needs: location, size, tuition costs, sport, division, and academics (grades, class rank, SAT/ACT). You personalize the list.

College Sports Questionnaire Samples

Here's a sample baseball questionnaire from Marietta College, a Division III school.

Full name (last, first, middle)			Known as		
Home address					Photo if available
Home phone	Date of birth	Date of grad.	High school coach		
Name of school	High school address		School enrollment		Brothers' names/ages
Father's name			Mother's name		
Occupation			Occupation		Sisters' names/ages
Employer			Employer		
Work phone			Work phone		
Hometown newspaper(s)					
Married Yes ( ) No ( )	What life's work are you preparing for? (teacher, coach, etc.)				

Number of students in class	Your rank in class		Attend any other college? Yes ( ) No( )	If yes, when and where?
SAT scores	Verbal	Math	If you haven't taken the SAT, when do you plan to?	High school cumulative grade average? 4.0 system
ACT composite score?	If you haven't taken the ACT, when do you plan to?		High school course of study (college prep, general, etc.)	

Ht.	Wt.	Bat R or L	Throw R or L	Est. of speed 40-yd. dash ___ 60 yd. dash ___	Arm MPH	Lettered varsity baseball years, incl. senior year
Positions (list in order of preference):					Team record last spring won lost	

STATISTICS FROM LAST SPRING

AB ( )   R ( )   H ( )   2B ( )   3B ( )   HR ( )   RBI ( )   BB ( )   SO ( )
SB ( )   BA ( )   PO ( )   ASST ( )   E ( )   DP ( )   FA ( )

PITCHING STATISTICS

GP ( )   IP ( )   H ( )   R ( )   ER ( )   ERA ( )   BB ( )   SO ( )
WON ( )   LOST ( )

Will you need financial aid to attend Marietta College? Yes ( ) No ( )

Have your parents submitted the FAFSA? This form is available at your high school.
Yes ( ) No ( )

When?   If not, please do so just as soon as possible!

Are you definitely interested in any other intercollegiate sports besides baseball?
Yes ( ) No ( )

If yes, which ones?

List any and all honors received for athletic and/or academic ability.

Who are the three best baseball players you have competed against, and who are still in high school?

	Name	Pos.	Year of grad.	High school name	Location (city/state)
1.					
2.					
3.					

Here's a sample questionnaire from Ohio University, a Divsion I school. Division I and II questionnaires tend to be similar.

Name_____ Soc. Sec. # _____

Street address _____ Phone _____

City_____ State_____ Zip _____

High school _____ Coach _____ Phone _____

Summer league team_____ Coach _____ Phone_____

Height_____Weight_____Birth date_____

Position _____ Throw: L   R   Bat: L   R

Mother's name _____ Occupation

Father's name_____ Occupation

Number of children in family_____#attending college_____# living at home_____

Baseball honors won_____

Other sports you participate in_____

Have you registered with the NCAA Clearinghouse?   Yes   No

Graduation date_____ Class rank_____ Out of_____

Have you completed the 13 academic course core curriculum as required for the NCAA Division I eligibility?   Yes   No   If NO, list the courses you will carry to complete this minimum requirement?

Core GPA_____ Over. GPA_____ ACT Comp._____ SAT. (v) _____(m)_____

College major you wish to study_____

Have your parents filled out a Financial Aid Form?   Yes   No

Have you applied for admission to Ohio University?   Yes   No

Have you applied for financial assistance, such as Ohio Institutional Grant or Basic Opportunity Grant?   Yes   No

Who was the best junior you played against last season?

1. _____ Position_____ High school_____ City_____

2. _____ Position_____ High School_____ City_____

Ohio University alumni or students you know:

Alumni_____Students_____

Videotaping Angles and Tips

If your finances are unlimited, you can sign up with a recruiting service to videotape your son or daughter's athletic performance to promote him/her, paying out as much as $2,500. If you're like the average parent who must watch the family finances, you can do it yourself for a whole lot less money.

In this chapter, you'll get lots of good information on ways to effectively videotape your student athlete so that you'll have good tapes to send to recruiting coaches. First we'll give you some general do's and don'ts; then we'll get specific in different sports' areas.

Keep these ideas in mind while filming your athlete:

1. Don't use too much "zoom" or you'll lose the revolving action.

2. Don't try to get closeups of the ball flying through the air.

3. Don't try to film through a fence or other obstruction. If there's no other choice, take your camera out of focus and use the manual feature. You'll be able to focus beyond the fence using this feature, but it's better to locate yourself somewhere else to avoid missing a shot because of an unfocused camera.

4. Don't film into direct sunlight because it will cause a glare on the camera lens that will record. Record with the sunlight either coming from behind or from the side.

5. Do use a tripod to avoid movement. Unstable camera work shows when producing a highlighted video.

6. Don't film at such a distance that you can't identify jersey numbers. If the camera doesn't show them, coaches won't know who's who.

7. Do record 10 seconds before and after you do an interview if you want to put in special effects.

8. Do start over if your prospect become tongue-tied during an interview, but keep the camera rolling to assure no glitches. You can always have it edited out.

9. Do purchase a very high-quality recording tape to record on.

10. Don't *ever* record on a tape that's already been recorded on.

Baseball

PITCHER   Angles: front, side, back

Camera/tripod staging areas: Stage your camera halfway between first base and home; halfway between third base and home; outfield (use zoom) as close to center field as possible; behind the catcher and offset yourself inside the fence; during drill sessions, stage yourself 15-20 feet within the pitcher's entire diameter; also capture shots from the catcher's view.

Primary/ key plays: Focus on accurate throws, at least five of each variety of pitches, ability to hustle and assist in fielding bunted balls, cutoff throws, pick-off plays to bases, ability to catch pop-ups and ground balls, and ability to help the catcher during a home steal situation.

CATCHER   Angles: Back, front, side

Camera/tripod staging areas: Stage your camera inside the fence and offset behind the catcher or umpire; halfway between home and first base; halfway between home and third base; during drill sessions, offset the camera/tripod behind pitcher

Primary/key plays: Focus on consistency of catching the ball, framing the pitch, accurate arm throw to second/third bases, area halfway between home and third base, catching pop-up balls, hustling to field bunted balls and on top of ground balls, covering the base during a runner coming home, making the tag, and blocking balls in the dirt.

SHORT STOP   Angles: front, left and right sides

Camera/tripod staging areas: Stage your camera parallel and offset 5-10 feet from first base; parallel and offset 5-10 feet from third base

Primary/key plays: Focus on hustling ability, accuracy on diving and making the catch, pop-ups and ground balls, accurate throwing arm and skill with making the out, cutoffs from the infield, double plays, lateral movement to both sides, and making tags.

OUTFIELDERS   Angles: front, left and right sides

Camera/tripod staging areas: Stage camera parallel and offset 5-10 feet from first base along the baseline; parallel and offset 5-10 feet from third base along the baseline; use zoom feature to stay clearly on the outfielder; once the catch is made, follow the throw of your prospect to the infield.

Primary/key plays: Focus on running ability, accurate judgment on making the catch; vertical leaping ability towards the back fence; lateral movement to both sides fielding fly balls, line drives, and ground balls; ability to place the ball in the infield using minimum time; hitting cutoff man; and throwing home from at least 250 feet.

FIRST BASE Angles: parallel, side, front

Camera/tripod staging areas: Stage your camera 10-15 feet behind first base; inside the diamond to the right of the catcher (don't capture the fence!); use zoom feature, keeping prospect clear and in focus at all times.

Primary/key plays: Focus on accurate and consistent catching ability, looking for that "reach out" position, ability to throw to other bases for a possible out, ability to tag leadoff runner, ability to assist and follow through with the double play, ability to catch pop-ups and ground balls, and catch balls in the dirt.

SECOND BASE Angles: parallel, side, front

Camera/tripod staging areas: Stage your camera halfway between third base and home; halfway between first base and home; use zoom feature; keep prospect clear and in focus at all times.

Primary/key plays: Focus on ability to make double plays, making the catch and tagging out the runner trying to steal second, tagging out the leadoff runner, working in conjunction with the shortstop, lateral movement, catching pop-ups and ground balls, catching incoming balls from the outfield, and consistency in throwing and catching.

THIRD BASE Angles: parallel, side, front

Camera/tripod staging areas: Stage your camera 10-15 feet behind third base; inside the diamond; to the left of the catcher (don't catch the fence!); use zoom feature, keeping your prospect clear and in focus at all times.

Primary/key plays: Focus on consistency with accurate catching and throwing ability, catching pop-up fly balls and ground balls, ability to tag out a runner trying to steal third, ability to tag out a leadoff, and fielding bunts.

Basketball

ALL POSITIONS   Angles: front, back, side

Camera/tripod staging areas: During drills, stage yourself on the court to get the full spectrum of your prospect. During dribbling drills, you want to show a closer view of the prospect to capture style and footwork while dribbling. During games, elevate yourself somewhere at half court; you want to capture your prospect offensively and defensively. The half-court advantage will allow you to utilize your zoom feature and maintain direct focus on your prospect. Remember, basketball contains a lot of running. It's vital to keep your prospect in the center of your lens, maintaining constant focus and zooming to distinguish your prospect's jersey number.

Primary/key plays: Focus on drills, filming all shooting positions: lay-ups, free throws, three-pointers, two-pointers, dribbling, etc. During games, keep the camera rolling at all times. Film all action that your prospect is involved in: offensive and defensive rebounds, dribbling, stealing, passing, shooting, defending, etc.

Football

OFFENSIVE AND DEFENSIVE LINE Angles: front, side, back

Camera/tripod staging areas: During games, stage yourself close to the press box or elevation somewhere along the 50-yard line. Utilize your zoom from this area and maintain a clear perspective of your prospect at all times. Be sure that jersey numbers are clear and distinguishable. During drills, place yourself where you can capture all angles, 20-30 feet from your prospect. Capture all detailed drills: sprints, blocking, tackling, sled pushing, scrimmage games, etc.

Primary/key plays: Seek out all of the action around and involving your prospect, capture all blocks or tackles, hustle ability, inside moves, and strength moves, look for pulling and double teaming, pass protection and blitz penetration, ability to stop the run, and all containing abilities.

CORNER BACK, SAFETY, AND LINEBACKER Angles: front, side, back

Camera/tripod staging areas: During games, try to stage yourself close to the press box or elevated area somewhere along the 50-yard line. Use your zoom from this area and maintain a clear perspective of your prospect at all times. Be sure that jersey numbers are clear and distinguishable at all times! During drills, stage yourself so that you can capture all angles 20-30 feet from your prospect. Capture all detailed drills: sprints, pursuit ability, reading the ball ability, tackling ability, hustle and interception ability, and scrimmage games.

Primary/key plays: Seek out all action around and involving your prospect; capture all pass coverage and tackles during pressure situations; stay focused on your prospect; show hustle ability, inside and outside moves, pursuing ability to stop the run, ability to read and intercept the pass, and all containing abilities.

WIDE RECEIVER, RUNNING BACK, TAIL BACK, OFFENSIVE END   Angles: front, side, back

Camera/tripod staging areas: During games, stage yourself close to the press box or elevated area along the 50-yard line. Use your zoom, maintaining a clear perspective of your prospect at all times. Be sure that jersey numbers are clear and distinguishable. During drills, situate yourself to capture all angles 20-30 feet from your prospect for sprints, running, ball handling, and scrimmage games.

Primary/key plays: Seek out all action around and involving your prospect, all inside and outside moves, running ability, running through the hole, breaking and shaking tackles, pass catching ability, the reverse, blocking, the big play, and getting into the end zone.

QUARTERBACK   Angles: front, side, back

Camera/tripod staging areas: During games, stage yourself close to the press box or elevation somewhere along the 50-yard line. Use your zoom, maintaining a clear perspective of your prospect at all times. Be sure that the jersey number is clear and distinguishable. During drills, capture all angles, 20-30 feet from your prospect and all detailed drills: sprints, passing, hand offs, and scrimmage games.

Primary/key plays: Focus on execution, hustling ability, fake-out moves, hand-offs, shuffle passes, screen passes, long passes, footwork, and ability to find the open man.

ALL KICKING POSITIONS   Angles: front, side, back

Camera/tripod staging areas: During games, try to stage yourself close to the press box or elevated area somewhere along the 50-yard line. Utilize your zoom, maintaining a clear perspective of your prospect at all times. Be sure that jersey numbers are clear and distinguishable. During drills, place yourself where you can capture all angles, about 20 feet from your prospect. Capture all detailed drills: field goals, punts, kickoffs, and scrimmage games. Stage yourself behind the kicker to capture the entire kick with the ball traveling through the arches. Also stage yourself behind the goal post. Be sure to maintain a distance far enough to capture the kick, rise, and execution of the ball traveling through the entire goal post.
Primary/key plays: Watch for proper execution and connection of all extra points, kickoffs, and punts.

Golf

GOLFERS   Angles: front, side, back

Camera/tripod staging areas: From the tee, stage yourself 20 feet directly in front of your prospect. This will allow you to capture the entire swing, showing full form. Remember to keep the camera rolling, and don't edit out any swings. Also stage yourself parallel and to the back of the tee. At this angle, you'll capture all entities of the back swing. You also will show how straight your prospect is actually hitting. From the green, stage yourself so that you can capture the full putt. From the sand trap, your staging area will vary. It's very important to film your prospect's full swing in the sand trap; then follow the ball to wherever it goes on the green.

Primary/key plays: If filming at a driving range, capture all strokes, using a variety of irons, woods, and drivers. If at a practice putting green, capture a variety of distance variance shots. If filming your prospect during a round of golf, film every stroke made by the prospect; include shots from the fairway to the sand trap.

Soccer

GOALIE Angles: front, side, back

Camera/tripod staging areas: During games inside a stadium, elevate yourself parallel and forward of the goal that your prospect is guarding. At this angle, you can capture all of the action that is taking place around the goal at a side view. Another angle that turns out very well is to stage your tripod and camera directly behind the goal.

Remember to stay at just enough distance to capture a few yards of the goal on both sides. At this angle, you can get a closer view, and by using your zoom, you can capture more action of the goalie. The same principles apply to games played in open fields. Since you can't elevate your camera, make everyone aware of who you are and what you're doing. Perhaps you'll have no trouble getting close to the field to stage your camera accordingly. During drills, try to capture a much closer view of your prospect. Move around to capture all defensive moves of the goalie.

Primary/key plays: Focus on blocks, saves, vertical leaping, diving, and hustling.

ALL OPEN FIELD POSITIONS   Angles: front, side, back

Camera/tripod staging areas: During games inside a stadium, elevate yourself along midfield. At this angle, you can follow your prospect with your zoom throughout the entire field. It's important to maintain focus and be close enough to read jersey numbers at all times. Soccer is solely a running and high endurance sport; you'll be very busy keeping your prospect in focus.

If your prospect is playing on an open soccer field, you may have to stage your camera/tripod directly somewhere midfield along the sideline. You'll be closer to all of the action if you're staged along the sideline at midfield. At this angle, go for the closer shots. Don't try to film the entire field! Follow the action of your prospect as it happens.

Primary/key plays: Focus on breaks, steals, passes, blocks, vertical leaps, sprints, traps, and goals.

Swimming and Diving

SWIMMERS   Angles: front, side

as close to the finish line as possible. When the race begins, you want to follow the prospect from start to finish. Your primary concern is to show the prospect's form. Don't try to film every competitor across the entire diameter of the swimming pool. Keep your prospect in the center of your lens so you'll capture good shots of the start, turns, and the finish.

Primary/key plays: Focus on starts, turns, and finishes.

DIVING   Angles: front, side, back

Camera/tripod staging areas: Camera placement will vary, so stage your camera as close to the diving area as possible. Form and water entry are the primary concerns with this sport. Once you stage your camera, start recording your prospect the moment he/she touches the ladder and don't stop until the prospect leaves the water.

Primary/key plays: Film all diving during all events, including practice.

Track and Field

SPRINTERS AND RELAY RACERS   Angles: front, side

Camera/tripod staging areas: Stage your camera as close as possible to the finish line. When filming any type of race, you want to freely use your zoom feature. If you're staged near the finish line, use your zoom and follow your prospect from start to finish. Keep the prospect in the center of your lens at all times. In sprint races, you can position yourself to the side of the starting line. This angle will allow you to get a good shot of the prospect's starts. During practice is the best time to film starts.

Primary/key plays: Film the entire race.

ALL FIELD EVENTS Angle: side

Camera/tripod staging areas: Try to place yourself parallel to wherever the action will take place. The geographical layout for all track and field meets may vary, so try to position your camera as close as you can to the prospect, using your best judgment. For all of the selected events, try to use your zoom lens and maintain a steady shot for that particular event.

Primary/key plays: Film the entire event.

Photo by Memory Lane Photography

Volleyball

ALL POSITIONS Angles: front, side, back

Camera/tripod staging areas: During practice, stage your camera center court on the opposing side. At this angle, you can film a variety of jumps, setups, and spikes. Also, stage your camera on the same side in one of the back corners of the court. You should be able to film defensive skills (saves and digs) better at this angle.

Stage your camera at the net, filming on the same side as the prospect. At this angle, try to film a closer view of your prospect. Using the zoom feature; try to pick up more detailed shots. During a game, elevate yourself as parallel to the net as possible. At this angle, you can film all relative action that involves your prospect.

Primary/key plays: Focus on spikes. saves, all hits, digs, kills, dives, blocks, and serves.

Wrestling

WRESTLERS   Angles: front, side, back

Camera/tripod staging areas: Stay at ground level as close to the wrestling mat as possible. You can clearly capture all action at this angle. Staging yourself next to the mat will ensure no obstructions. When filming from this area, keep the camera rolling at all times, maintaining a steady shot. You also can film from the bleachers if you're elevated. Use your zoom feature. Although this angle is good, we recommend shooting as close as possible to the mat. Capture only the wrestling match containing your prospect. If you can film the prospect during practice, capture shots of take downs, reverses, pinning combination moves, and escapes.

Primary/key plays: Film the entire match.

How to Find Valuable Contacts

Ask questions! Valuable contacts aren't going to come to you, but they may be nearby! They can be anywhere. They can be coaches, players, parents, guidance counselors, or anybody you think is knowledgeable about the schools you may attend. Ask if they know any current or former coaches or players at these colleges. Once you've narrowed your choices, connect with current or former players, alumni, or friends of the coaches or athletes they coached earlier in their careers. Find out as much as you can about the coach's background, such as what high school or college he/she attended.

Additional credible sources will be an opposing coach, a current or former college or pro athlete (advice from a person who's played the game in a higher division level will usually be more valuable than one who hasn't), and your high-school coach if he/she has a good collegiate background in sports or a good relationship with college coaches. Ask coaches of other sports in your high school about their college experiences, especially if they went to the colleges you're considering.

Radio

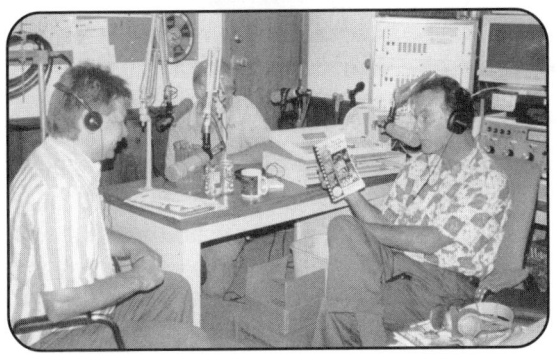

John "Cappy" Caparanis, radio talk show host of ESPN Sports Radio 1240 AM, interviews Bercik about the recruiting process that leads to athletic scholarships.

Read sports pages in the newspapers, talk to sportswriters, listen to local sports radio shows (usually on AM) and watch TV sports shows, call the sports radio and TV broadcasters to find out who's attended/attending the colleges you're interested in, work out at a local gym and network there, talk to people at sports events, check college rosters for players from your area, talk to the sports information director at a college for info about the coach and players, and look on the internet for websites and rosters of teams.

Keep your eyes and ears open at all times for those who can recommend you. Get names, addresses, and phone numbers for references. Provide your reference person with a self-addressed stamped envelope, along with the name and address of the coach on the envelope. Include all accurate information about yourself.

TV

Mike Case, TV NBC Sports anchor for the weekly high-school football show called "Inside High-school Football," interviews the author about the recruiting process that leads to athletic scholarships.

The bottom line is: the more times your name is heard through good reference by a college coach, the better your chances of being noticed and having that coach come to see you play.

All photos in this section will give you an example of how many valuable contacts can come to your city or vicinity. Each of these pictures was taken within a radius of 20 miles from my hometown.

Many valuable contacts are within your reach, too; you just need to know where to look for the information about when and where they will visit your area.

Remember that a valuable contact doesn't always have to be somebody who can possibly help you get a scholarship. It can be somebody who can help you get a better understanding of what collegiate and professional sports are actually like. A good example is to be able to listen to a former or current athlete speak of his/her experiences at a sports-related banquet or scholarship dinner.

The photos on the next page were taken at only one sports banquet. It should give you an idea of how relaxed the settings are at these gatherings.

Sports Banquets

Elvis Grbac, (R), former quarterback for the San Francisco 49ers and Baltimore Ravens and former University of Michigan teammate, John Kolesar, (C) with a father and his son at the Warren Sports "Hall of Fame" dinner in Warren, Ohio.

(L-R) Tim Davis, former University of Michigan nose guard; the author; Ray Griffin, former defensive back at the Ohio State University, the Cincinnati Bengals, and the Buffalo Bills; and Aaron Brown, former defensive end for the Ohio State University and the Tampa Bay Buccanneers.

Howard "Hopalong" Cassidy (R), Heisman Trophy halfback for the Ohio State University, with Allison Gatta, publicist for *America's Complete SPORTS SCHOLARSHIP GUIDE.*

Former athletes, not just the ones pictured, don't hesitate to answer any question that a young athlete or his/her parents may have if approached before or after the banquet. These former athletes view these opportunities as a way of *giving something back to the game.*

Scholarship Dinners

Paul Maguire (L), ESPN NFL analyst and former professional football player from the Citadel University, with the author at the Nick Johnson Scholarship Dinner created by Paul to benefit student-athletes from his alma mater Ursuline High School in Youngstown, Ohio,

Bob Stoops (L), head football coach for the University of Oklahoma 2000 National Championship Team and the 2000 college football "Coach of the Year," with the author at the Cardinal Mooney High School Athletic Hall of Fame Banquet and Ron Stoops Scholarship Dinner in Youngstown, Ohio.

Fund-raising Banquets

The author (L) gets an autograph from Archie Griffin, associate athletic director at the Ohio State University and the only two-time Heisman Trophy winner, at an Easter Seals fund-raising banquet in Youngstown, Ohio.

Jim Tressel (R), the 2002 college football "Coach of the Year" of the Ohio State University Buckeyes' 2002 national championship team, autographs a football at a fund-raising banquet for Heart Reach Ministries that helps underprivileged youngsters in Youngstown, Ohio.

Autograph Signings

Matt Wilhelm, All-American linebacker for the Ohio State Buckeyes' 2002 national championship team, autographs a picture for nine-year-old Joey Tuchek, as his father, Joe (R), and Ken Kollar (C), general manager of the Eastwood Mall in Niles, Ohio, look on.

Kelly Holcomb, Cleveland Browns quarterback (C), with "Mr. Sports" (R), the disc jockey for Y-103 Radio in Yongstown, Ohio, and youngsters Ronnie Haun, (L) and Scott Batcho (R), at an autograph signing promoted by Y-103 for the area's Cleveland Browns fans at the Saturn car dealership in Niles, Ohio.

Sports Camps

All pictures on this page were taken at the **Camp of Champions Summer Football camp for youngsters (grades 3-8) held at Cardinal Mooney High School in Youngstown, Ohio.** Campers Joey Kirila (L) and Marcus Yensick (R) with Bob Stoops, head football coach for the University of Oklahoma (L); Mike Stoops, associate head football coach for the University of Oklahoma (C); and Bernie Kosar, former quarterback for the Cleveland Browns and the University of Miami, Florida (R).

Mark "Bo" Pelini, defensive coordinator for the University of Nebraska.

Mark Stoops, defensive backs coach for the University of Miami, Florida

Michael Zordich, Philadelphia Eagles and Penn State All-American defensive back.

Gino Toretta, the 1992 Heisman Trophy winner from the University of Miami, Florida.

Photo by John Young

Local Athletic Clubs

This section was designed to show just how many opportunities are out there to find valuable contacts. These photos were all taken within a 20-mile radius of my hometown with all but a few taken during the course of one year and the rest within a two-year period.

The same kind of functions and opportunities occur regularly in any areas–you just need to keep your eyes and ears open and take advantage of what is going on around you. Your valuable contact may not be even be the one you are going to see or listen to, but it may be another person who appears at one of these sports-related funtions. And when you come face-to-face with a potential valuable contact, it's up to you to present yourself and your situation. Will you be prepared to intoduct yourself and communicate your wishes/ideas/intentions when that time comes? You may get only one chance to get that person's attention and to sell yourself, so be prepared to do so in a brief amount of time. What will you say or ask that will be both interesting and informative to him/her and benefit you?

John "Cappy" Caparanis, ESPN Sports Radio 1240 AM with Jack Kucek (L), former Chicago White sox pitcher, and Frank Derry (C) editor and publisher of *Bernie's Insiders and Indians Ink,* football and baseball professional sports magazines at the Trumbull County Athletic Hall of Fame's monthly gathering called "Speaking of Sports" at the Ground Round in Warren, Ohio.

Photo by John Young

(L-R) Bob Stoops, head football coach, University of Oklahoma; Mark Stoops, defensive backs coach, University of Miami, Florida; Ed Muransky, former Oakland Raider lineman from the University of Michigan; and Mike Stoops, associate head football coach, University of Oklahoma, at the Cardinal Mooney alumni fundraising dinner at the MVR Club in Youngstown, Ohio.

ADVICE FROM

"THE MEDIA"

Advice from Budd Bailey, Sports Department, *Buffalo News*

Budd Bailey has worked for the sports department of the Buffalo News *since 1994. Before that, he was director of information for the Buffalo Sabres and served as a talk show host and reporter for WEBR Radio in Buffalo, New York. Budd is the author of* Celebrate the Tradition, *a history of the Buffalo Sabres.*

I have worked in a variety of jobs with connections to the media over the years. I've covered high school, college, and professional events for radio. I've worked in public relations in pro sports. I've written and edited for weekly and daily newspapers. I've done some free-lance writing for magazines. I've even done a little television work.

So let me assure you that when I say one of the most difficult jobs in the media is to cover high-school sports for a big-city newspaper, I've got a good reason. And that reason comes down to one word: parents.

I fully realize what sort of pressure parents are under these days when it comes to helping their children go to college. The costs of higher education keep going up and up, making it more difficult to afford it. There are athletic scholarships out there, but the demand is much greater than the supply.

Plenty of parents think members of the media can punch tickets to scholarships for their children. So they call the reporter and complain than John or Jane Doe was the subject of a big article in today's paper, but he or she isn't half the player that their son or daughter is.

Their frustration is easily understood, and their concern is admirable. They are dreaming of a better life for their children. But their perspective is wrong. They are working in the wrong way, and their eagerness tends to alienate the very person who can give a child's scholarship chances a very small boost by helping to pick all-conference teams. One of my coworkers received so many complaint calls from parents that he simply gave up writing articles about virtually all individual high-school athletes; it just wasn't worth the trouble.

As you'll read in this book, the process of getting a scholarship starts with two vital points: athletics and academics. A student athlete has to have both. Athletic skills are obviously important because coaches are under pressure themselves to recruit players who can help them win.

But academics are just as important. The landscape is littered with players who had all the talent in the world to play college sports but didn't have the grades. If you'd like some examples, go to the library and read Darcy Frey's excellent *The Last Shot*, about basketball players from the projects of Coney Island, who in some cases didn't have the SAT scores to get into college.

If those two cornerstones are in place, then you can work on the other areas. If the question is, "How do I get my child some exposure among recruiters?", the answer has a variety of aspects. Today's athletes should attend all of the camps and clinics they can. It's a great way to improve their skills, be seen by potential coaches, and build up a reputation in the community. You can't beat a personal relationship.

Your VCR can be an important tool. Many local cable systems broadcast high-school games on local access channels. Tape your child's games and build a library. Your child should be watching his or her play to see how he or she can improve anyways, and you'll also have tapes in case a recruiter is interested enough to want to see more. If television isn't an option, you might want to consider buying a camcorder.

Then there's the 21st century method – the internet. Your school or league may have a website dedicated to it. You can make sure that the site has up-to-date, accurate information on it, so that it can become a useful tool for anyone who cares to visit it.

If today's high school athlete follows those steps and is good enough, the media will notice him or her. It may start with a simple few words about a particular game in the newspaper and grow into full feature-length articles in the newspaper or stories on television news programs.

An interview with a member of the media can be a nerve-wracking experience for anyone who isn't used to it. Imagine what's it's like for someone who is 16 years old or so. I've talked to many student athletes over the years, and I can think of two tips for them:

1. Learn how to express yourself. The reporter is looking for as much information as possible. If he or she asks, "How did it feel to hit that game-winning homer?", don't answer "Great" and wait for the next question. You could say something like, "It was great. I knew I had to stay calm in that situation and wait for a pitch I could hit." Listen to how professional athletes answer questions; they have gone through this drill before. Giving good answers is not easy and may require some practice, but it will be a big help when you are faced with this situation.

2. Have fun. You aren't giving the State of the Union address. It's a thrill to see your name in the newspaper or see yourself on the 11 o'clock news. Treat it that way. Let your personality come out a little.

It's nice to have those articles in a scrapbook, and recruiters have their memories jogged if they happen to see story about a promising student athlete. But keep this in perspective – the media has a very small role in the process today. College scholarships don't go to the students with the most press clippings. They go to the best athletes.

Anyone who has ever played sports while growing up has wished he or she could earn an athletic scholarship to college. Just remember that the winners usually spent as much time hitting the books as hitting a baseball or softball. But remember, dreams can come true.

Advice from Greg Gulas, Sportswriter, Former S. I. D.

Greg is a former sports information director at Youngstown State University who was a four-year baseball player at YSU as an undergraduate. A former college coach at YSU, Greg is now a sportswriter for *The Vindicator* and the *Boardman News* in Youngstown, Ohio.

Q: **What are the responsibilities of a sports information director?**

A: The responsibilities are to disseminate to the media all information on all sports and squads playing both men's and women's sports at the institution that you represent. We do features on the players and coaches and update statistics, as well as reporting actual game results if they can't be covered by the actual media representative.

Q: What advice do you have for student athletes and the parents on the athletic recruiting process?

A: As a former sports information director, I feel it's important first to know all about the school for what you plan to major in. Then get to know the coach and see if there's a genuine warmth that he brings to the position he holds. You're there to get an education first and then play sports, but you want to feel comfortable in all aspects of the collegiate experience.

As a sportswriter, I feel that the student athlete should feel comfortable at the games and practices when media members are present. They're there to report on your team, so feel comfortable talking to them. Again, get to know the sports information director and his staff so that not only can you help them out but also they, in turn, will cover you in a first-class manner.

Q: What are the most important factors you believe that student athletes should be aware of in the transition from high school to the collegiate sports level?

A: Making new friends is something that takes place naturally. Classes and homework will consume much more of your time during your scholastic days, so learn to alter your schedule and make good use of your spare time. Learning to budget your time among classes, homework, rest, and your sport is most critical if you are to survive. Good grades keep you eligible, so remember to make sure you understand the true meaning of the term "student athlete." A student first—athlete second!

Q: What experience and advice can you share with student athletes and parents concerning the benefits of knowing alumni from the college you may consider attending?

A: Having an alumnus write you a letter of recommendation or calling the coach can give you the edge over your competition that you need when it comes to athletic recruiting. The college coaches choose from hundreds of prospects each year; you can use all the help you can get.

As a sports information director, I never know who I can help out. It's a great idea to get to know as many alumni as you possibly can as they're the ones out there in the job world, and it's very helpful when it comes time to look for a job. In the recruiting process, a coach taps all of his resources to get to the athlete to convince him/her that his/her school is the place to pursue an academic/athletic career.

As a sportswriter, I want to know the alumni because they can help me when I need to get to a source, to confirm or deny anything about a story. While out of the limelight, the alumni still want to be a part so what better way than to include their names in your article, hoping down the line they'll remember and help you with your source.

Q: How would you suggest student athletes find alumni contacts who may be able to help get his/her name "heard"?

A: As a SID, I suggest that you stop by the alumni office or talk to a coach for a listing of all the letter winners in their sport, complete with addresses and phone numbers for contacts.

As a sportswriter, I suggest you get to know the beat writer, as he's seen many alumni come and go and probably keeps in touch with them. He can be a valuable resource when trying to find alumni.

Q: How would you suggest student athletes research their future competition at colleges they're considering attending? For example, how do they find out who was recruited last year, who walked on, who transferred, what positions the team may be recruiting for this upcoming season?

A: As a SID, I suggest seeing the coach or stopping by the SID office to get past and future schedules so that they can see the type of competition that the team has been playing. Then decide if that is the level of competition they want to compete at.

As a sportswriter, I suggest you get old articles and read about the type of competition that the school has been playing and the sports in which they compete.

Trying to make a deadline–all in a days work. Greg puts his college education (B.A. in speech and drama and M.A. in English/Sports Administration) to good use as a sportswriter for the newspaper.

PARENTS'

SECTION

Preparing Your Child for College Isn't an Easy Matter

Unless you're independently wealthy and can hire somebody to work out the details of sending your son or daughter off to college, you have a lot of work ahead of you.

Some of the tasks ahead of you can seem overwhelming, but if you take it step by step by reading and asking lots of questions of lots of people, everything will fall into place—sooner or later!

Some advice: Keep in mind that college isn't for everyone!

Once you and your child have decided that college *is* in the picture, you need to methodically go about your planning, using the journalistic "who, what, why, where, when, and how" principle to make decisions.

You can eliminate "who" because we already know "who."

"What" might refer to a course of study/major/degree that's offered at a school that also offers the sport your child wants to participate in. Remember that some young folks don't really have an agenda for the future when they begin college, and that's OK, too. "What" might also refer to "What's involved in finding out all about the school, the athletic program, the study requirements, etc." This is where you take advantage of the school guidance counselors' expertise, other people who've already been through this scenario, the public library, and the internet with its wealth of easily accessible information.

A great website that will help you immensely is http://www.ed.gov/pubs/prepare/. The table of contents lets you plug into general questions about college—how to choose one, financing a college education, important terms to understand, exercises and checklists, and ten different charts of different topics. Charts include examples of jobs requiring college preparation, questions to ask guidance counselors, typical college costs, average tuition and fees, military postsecondary education opportunities, and more.

"Why" is self-explanatory. Your child wants to engage in a sport and earn a degree at the same time so he/she can support him/herself after college, whether it's in the business world or in the sports arena. Your question might be: "Why do you want to go to this particular school?"

"Where" points back to the particular school. You have to calculate the cost of not only the education but also the travel expenses for all of you, new wardrobes if the climate is totally different, transportation for the student, etc., "Where" covers a lot of territory, so to speak, and you'll have to come up with your own questions regarding where your child goes to school.

"When" isn't as simple as it seems. While most high-school graduates go off to college the next fall, some just aren't ready to take that step just then. Or perhaps you don't have all of the financial bugs worked out. Nothing is written in stone that everybody *has* to start the September after high-school graduation.

And then we come to "How." This is the biggie, and most of it concerns finances in one form or another. How much does it cost to go to school? How can I afford it? How do we get financial aid? How do we apply for student loans? The "hows" go on and on.

Our advice? Just don't wait till the last minute, and don't put all of the burden of finding out what needs to be understood on your child. Get involved yourself so that you completely understand what you need to know.

Another helpful website is www.asep.com/asep/parents. Take this recruiting guide with you to your local library if you don't have a home computer, and don't forget the site on the previous page.

Where Can You Find Out about Scholarships?

Although searching for scholarship information by way of the computer is quick, free, and easy, there are other places to look, too. Investigate local community and civic resources. Check the churches, synagogues, or local organizations with which you may be affiliated. Check with the personnel office of your employer or even grandparents' employers to see if they offer any scholarships for which your child may be qualified. Contact national organizations that may offer scholarships to individuals with your cultural background, personal circumstances, and skills. Have your child discuss the scholarship search with the high-school guidance counselors, faculty members, and college/university staff. Check with the college academic department to locate information regarding national professional organizations with scholarship programs.

Remember: It takes time and effort to see results from your scholarship search, but you must always remain positive. Never give up on your search for free money that can assist with college expenses.

Check your public library for these and other books:

Blum, Laurie. *Free Money from Colleges and Universities.* New York: H. Holt and Co., 1993.

Cassidy, Daniel J. *The Scholarship Book*, second edition. Englewood Cliffs, NJ: Prentice Hall, 1984.

Foundation Grants to Individuals, eighth edition. New York: The Foundation Center, 1993.

Paying Less for College, 13th edition. Princeton, NJ: Peterson's Guides, 1996.

Advice from Walter Kohowski: Athletic Recruiting—a Father's Observations

I'm a 46-year-old father of two boys, Michael and Patrick. My oldest has just graduated from high school and gone through the athletic recruiting process for football. I'm a former high-school athlete, an Ohio State University graduate, and a sandlot baseball coach. I relate this bit of my own history so that you'll have a better understanding of my feelings regarding college recruiting.

I think that every parent who has a child participating in high-school athletics dreams of the "big time" for their son or daughter. What they need to realize is that the percentage of high-school athletes who go on to play, and I emphasize "play," at Division I schools is very low. What the student athletes need to determine is whether or not they want to continue on in the sport. *The emphasis needs to be put on "student"—not "athlete."*

As I mentioned before, my oldest son has just finished the recruiting process, and I can honestly say that I enjoyed it as much as he did. Michael was a two-time All-Conference performer and an honorable mention All-State selection in Ohio while playing for Youngstown Cardinal Mooney High School. He was recruited by numerous Division III schools (they aren't permitted to give out athletic scholarships or athletic aid).

At first, Michael read the letters and talked to different coaches via phone. Most, if not all, kept in touch during his season. After the season was over and Michael had the chance to talk to his guidance counselor and his own coaches, he decided on the schools he wanted to visit. Every weekend, he and I were on the go; the visits were usually the same: a tour of the campus and the athletic facilities, talks with players, coaches, faculty members, etc. The head coach usually sums up the visit and explains to the parents what the school can do for you financially. College is very expensive and coaches realize it. They also realize that parents become very anxious when college costs are discussed.

I was pleasantly surprised when topics of discussion contained accessibility to churches; different types of leisure activities; and most important, the focus on education; what each school would provide for my son for his future; the commitments they'd make so that he'd be successful. His athletic career would be secondary to his education.

To be honest, I want Michael to enjoy his college years; they're just as formative as his years prior to college. He'll have the chance to become a man on his own without my interference. He'll have a chance to make his own life-changing decisions. What I expect from his college is the opportunities to be present for Michael to make those decisions.

Author's note: *While discussing financial aid with Walter, we talked about a severance pay he'd received from his former employer. The financial aid officer determined that this was a "special circumstance" in that it raised his income that year but wouldn't continue to do so. Clearing up that matter helped Walter get more financial aid for his son. Remember to be clear and concise when giving information to the financial aid people. And always remember to ask about the Regional Service Area discount if your son or daughter will attend a school within a certain radius of your home.*

Advice from Shirley Libeg, Athletic Recruiting—a Mother's Observations

As the mother of three sons and whose youngest child went through the recruiting process in baseball last year, I feel qualified to discuss this issue from a "motherly" perspective.

My son, who played for Hubbard High School in Ohio, had a very successful high school career in baseball and basketball. If a high-school student desires to play a sport on the college level, it is imperative that he or she be involved in extra-curricular activities while in high school. Participating in clubs, holding offices, and doing volunteer work are a few of the activities that should be encouraged. Most important of all, however, is for a student to excel in his/her studies, earn high grades in school, and perform well on the SAT or ACT tests. If a student is having difficulty with the standardized tests, he/she should seek tutorial help either through the school or from a private source. After the junior year, it is a good idea to have your son/daughter prepare a resume of all high-school activities in preparation for the recruiting process.

In our son's case, he began to receive calls and questionnaires from colleges in the fall of his senior year. While he did have the desire and capabilities to attend a Division I school, we also visited a few Division III schools that proved to be very enlightening to us. It was interesting to visit the schools and meet with the different coaches, who were all very cordial and willing to share valuable information with us. I enjoyed participating in this process, and it afforded us some "quality" time with our youngest son, who would soon be leaving for college.

At times, I found the whole process quite perplexing. While I never profess to fully understand all of the intricacies of baseball, I found it immensely enjoyable to visit these campuses and get a feel for the college life and academics at each one. After the campus tour, we would meet with the coaches, and they would explain how my son would fit into their baseball program.

Then the unexpected happened. My son had always planned to go away to school just as his older brothers did. We started getting calls from our local college. The coaches made an effort to make me, as well as my husband, feel like an integral part of this decision. My son narrowed his choices down two schools. At this time, it is extremely important for parents to provide guidance and support, but in the end, I feel that it comes down to these questions: 1. Does this school offer my field of study? 2. What is my opportunity with this athletic team? 3. Who wants me the most? 4. What are the financial considerations?

In the final analysis, my son chose to attend a college near home, and he lives in the dorm with the other baseball players. He is currently a freshman and after participating in an intensive fall weight-lifting program, he gained 15 pounds on his 6'4" frame.

The first semester of college is certainly a learning experience, and time management skills are necessary, especially when participating in a sport at a Division I college. The daily routine of practice, lifting, and study table requires much self-discipline and organization. As a mother, it's gratifying to see my son become an independent young man thriving in his academic and sports endeavors.

The recruiting process is certainly full of "ups" and "downs." There were disappointments, as well as pleasant surprises, along the way. There is no "right" way to get through this. I would encourage mothers to participate in what could be one of the most life-changing decisions of your son/daughter's life.

Advice from Financial Aid Advisors
Great Websites Provide a Wealth of Information

Ever want to find out whatever you could on the Internet but didn't know where to look? Well, we've done a lot of the hard work by finding valuable websites that promise to help you in many different areas of the college scene.

Again, we advise you to take this guide with you and plan to spend some time at the library on one of their computers if you don't have your own. If you do have a computer, set aside some time each day to look at these websites. We promise that you'll be glad you did. The information we're providing is recommended by Nina Conner, financial aid officer at Kent State University's Student Financial Aid Office Trumbull Branch.

COLLEGE INFORMATION

www.ed.gov (U. S. Department of Education)—This website will give you information on college costs at all colleges/universities for tuition and fees, room and board, books, and on- and off-campus living; courses and majors offered; enrollment; graduation rates; male-to-female and ethnic ratios; and crime statistics on campus.

www.collegeboard.org This site gives estimates of what four years of college will cost, assuming seven percent annual increases in college expenses. Also gives approximate monthly payment costs on Stafford Loans after graduation.

www.collegebound.net

www.collegeispossible.org

FINANCIAL AID INFORMATION

www.finaid.org Through this site, you'll have access to multiple databases for financial aid information, specific scholarship information, and links to other scholarship services

www.studentservices.com/fastweb This is a new and exciting World Wide Web computer resource. This product, FASTWEB, compares student information with 180,000 awards in the FASTWEB Student Services; database through the internet.

www.rams.com/wrn/ The Scholarship Resource Network is another World Wide Web computer resource, similar to FASTWEB in that it compares the student's information to their databases.

http://scholarships.salliemae.com (CASHE) An automated national database that provides resource information on scholarships, loans, and grants.

www.collegenet.com/mach25/ (NET MACH25) This site contains over 50,000 private sector awards, including institutional awards. Students can view the results of the database search, save information in their profile, and generate letters to the scholarship sponsor to request additional information. The database is updated annually.

www.gohotline.com/scholarship

www.college-scholarships.com/

www.scholarships.com

http://www.scholarship stuff.com

CAMPUS LIFE INFORMATION

www.gohotline.com/campus/ Links to campus newspapers in the U.S.

www.gohotline.com/fraternity/ Links to college fraternities

www.gohotline.com/sorority/ Links to college sororities

EDUCATIONAL INFORMATION

www.gohotline.com Links to numerous educational subjects

The U. S. Department of Education publishes a great financial aid guide, *The Student Guide*, that we highly recommend to answer your questions about topics such as eligibility, Pell Grants, and Stafford Loans. Have your son or daughter ask the guidance conselor for a copy or write to the Federal Student Aid Information Center, P. O. Box 84, Washington, D. C, 20044-0084 for your free copy.

NCAA ADVICE AND INFORMATION

Information from the *2003-04 NCAA Guide for the College-Bound Student-Athlete*

Information provided is subject to yearly change by the NCAA.

This is only an abbreviated version of all the rules and regulations that you need to know. Contact your high-school guidance counselor or visit the NCAA website www.ncaa.org for up-to-date material.

Student athletes must understand that the recruiting process starts with academics, and it begins in their freshmen year. If students don't meet NCAA academic and eligibility requirements, they will not receive sports scholarships regardless of their athletic ability."

**Mike Stoops,
associate head football coach,
University of Oklahoma, 2000 National Champions**

The National Collegiate Athletic Association has the say-so on competing in sports in college and stresses academics, as well as athletics. This organization doesn't discriminate against any person regardless of race, color, national origin, disability, gender, age with respect to its governance policies, educational programs, activities, and employment policies.

The NCAA does have rules and regulations for college athletes that must be adhered to regarding academic eligibility and employment policies.

Information in this chapter comes from the *2003-04 NCAA Guide for the College-Bound Student-Athlete* that you, as a future college student or parent of a college-bound athlete, absolutely need in order to understand NCAA policies. To get an online version of the complete NCAA guide, go to www.ncaaclearinghouse.net, or you can call their customer service line toll-free at 877/262-1492 between 8:00 a.m. and 5:00 p.m. Central Time, Monday-Friday. There is also a 24-hour Clearinghouse Hotline that you can call at 877/861-3003. And finally, the toll-free number for the Publications Division is 888/388-9748.

Academic Eligibility Requirements

Every student entering college is required to have taken core curriculum courses: English, natural or physical science, mathematics, social science, and some courses in humanities. Requirements regarding the number of years/credits for each subject vary within Divisions I, II, and III. Additionally, every student must have taken ACT and SAT tests and received a specified minimum score. GPAs are very important when entering or being accepted by any college or university.

Keep this thought in mind: no matter what school you attend or what major you choose, education is your first concern. Even though you enter college thinking that your choice may lead to a career in the pros, consider that

- there are nearly one million high-school football players and about 550,000 basketball players. Of that number, about 250 make it to the NFL and about 50 make an NBA team;

- less than three percent of college seniors will play one year in professional basketball; and

- the odds of a high-school football player making it to the pros at all—let alone having a career—are about 6,000 to 1; the odds for a high-school basketball player are 10,000 to 1.

Take a hard look at those numbers and think about what will matter in the long run—A COLLEGE EDUCATION!

IMPORTANT NEW INFORMATION! ABOUT NCAA ELIGIBILITY REQUIREMENTS

The NCAA Division I initial-eligibility rules have changed. If you plan to enroll in any college or university in fall 2003 or after, please read this information carefully.

For students entering any college or university during the 2003-04 or 2004-05 academic years, your initial eligibility will be evaluated under the new rule as described on the following pages. If you are ineligible under the new rule, the NCAA Initial-Eligibility Clearinghouse will automatically re-evaluate your academic record under the former rule to obtain your best possible result. It is not possible to mix-and-match rules. For example, you cannot use the 13-core course standard of the former rule and the sliding scale from the new rule.

For students entering any or college or university on or after August 1, 2005, your NCAA initial eligibility will be evaluated using the new rule only.

THE NEW RULE:

- increases the number of core courses from 13 to 14. This additional core course may be in any area. English, mathematics, natural/physical science, social science, foreign language, nondoctrinal religion/philosophy, or computer science. The breakdown of core course requirements is listed below.

- changes the Division I initial-eligibility index, or sliding scale. See the page following the new rules for the core courses for the Core GPA/test score sliding scale index

FORMER RULE	**NEW RULE**
13 Core Courses:	**14 Core Courses**
4 years of English	4 years of English.
2 years of mathematics (algebra 1 or higher)	2 years of mathematics (algebra 1 or higher).
2 years of natural/physical science (1 year of lab if offered by high school).	2 years of natural/physical science (1 year of lab if offered by high school).

1 year of additional English, mathematics or natural/physical science.	1 year of additional English, mathematics or natural/physical science.
2 years of social science.	2 years of social science.
2 years of additional courses (from any area above or foreign language, nondoctrinal religion/ philosophy, computer science*).	3 years of additional courses (from any area above or foreign language, nondoctrinal religion/ philosophy, computer science*).

Please note: Computer science is being eliminated as an acceptable core-course area for students first entering college or university on or after August 1, 2005. Students entering college on or after August 1, 2005, may not use any computer science courses in meeting core-course requirements.

Author's note: *Please take careful note of these changes to see which rule or index pertains to you.*

OTHER IMPORTANT INFORMATION

Effective date of new rule

- Students entering a collegiate institution on or after August 1, 2003, may meet the initial-eligibility requirements under either rule.

- Students first entering a collegiate institution on or after August 1, 2005, must meet the new 14-course rule.

For more information regarding the new rule, please go to www.ncaa.org. Click on "Custom Home Pages" and pull the menu down to "Prospect/Parent" page.

Division II is proposing an increase to 14-core courses. The additional course could be taken in any core-course area. The proposal if adopted, would be effective for students first entering a collegiate institution on or after August 1, 2005.

Below is the FORMER CORE GPA/Test Score Index
(to be used with 13-core courses)

Core GPA	ACT	SAT
2.500 and above	68	820
2.475	69	830
2.450	70	840-850
2.425	70	860
2.400	71	860
2.375	72	870
2.350	73	880
2.325	74	890
2.300	75	900
2.275	76	910
2.250	77	920
2.225	78	930
2.200	79	940
2.175	80	950
2.150	80	960
2.125	81	960
2.100	82	970
2.075	83	980
2.050	84	990
2.025	85	1000
2.000	86	1010

Below is the NEW CORE GPA/Test Score Index
(to be used with 14-core courses)

New Core GPA	ACT	SAT
3.550 and above	37	400
3.525	38	410
3.500	39	420
3.475	40	430
3.450	41	440
3.425	41	450
3.400	42	460
3.375	42	470
3.350	43	480
3.325	44	490
3.300	44	500
3.275	45	510
3.250	46	520
3.225	46	530

Below is the NEW CORE GPA/Test Score Index

Core GPA	ACT	SAT
3.200	47	540
3.175	47	550
3.150	48	560
3.125	49	570
3.100	49	580
3.075	50	590
3.050	50	600
3.025	51	610
3.000	52	620
2.975	52	630
2.950	53	640
2.925	53	650
2.900	54	660
2.875	55	670
2.850	56	680
2.825	56	690
2.800	57	700
2.775	58	710
2.750	59	720
2.725	59	730
2.700	60	730
2.675	61	740-750
2.650	62	760
2.625	63	770
2.600	64	780
2.575	65	790
2.550	66	800
2.525	67	810
2.500	68	820
2.475	69	830
2.450	70	840-850
2.425	70	860
2.400	71	860
2.375	72	870
2.350	73	880
2.325	74	890
2.300	75	900
2.275	76	910
2.250	77	920
2.225	78	930
2.200	79	940
2.175	80	950
2.150	80	960
2.125	81	960
2.100	82	970
2.075	83	980
2.050	84	990
2.025	85	1000
2.000	86	1010

DIVISION II REQUIREMENTS

If you're first entering a Division II college on or after August 1, 1996, in order to be classified a "qualifier," you're required to:

- graduate from high school;

- have a GPA of 2.000 (based on a maximum of 4.000) in a successfully completed core curriculum of at least 13 academic course units as follows:

- English...3 years

- mathematics...2 years

- natural or physical science (including at least one laboratory course, if offered by the high school............2 years

- additional courses in English, mathematics, or natural or physical science..2 years

- social science... 2 years

- additional academic courses in any of the above areas of foreign language, computer science*, philosophy or nondoctrinal religion, e.g., comparative religion courses..2 years

have a combined score on the SAT verbal and math sections 820 (if taken on or after April 1, 1995) or a 68 sum score on the ACT.

Division II is proposing an increase to 14-core courses. The additional course could be taken in any core-course area. The proposal if adopted, would be effective for students first entering a collegiate institution on or after August 1, 2005.

DIVISION III REQUIREMENTS

These requirements currently don't apply to Division III colleges, where eligibility for financial aid, practice, and competition is governed by institutional, conference, and other regulations.

Initial Eligibility Clearinghouse

No, this isn't Ed McMahon and the Publisher's Clearinghouse offering you a sweepstakes prize. It's the NCAA Central Clearinghouse that certifies your athletic eligibility for Divisions I and II. If you intend to participate in athletics as a freshman, you *must* register and be certified by the NCAA Initial-Eligibility Clearinghouse.

You must register by completing the student release form that's in the book and mailing it, along with a $30 registration fee.

The NCAA Clearinghouse has launched a series of services to support prospective student athletes. The key features of the new Clearinghouse include 1. A NCAA Clearinghouse website at www.ncaaclearinghouse.net (You may access the Clearinghouse home page directly or through links from NCAA's website: www.ncaa.org.), and 2. from the NCAA Clearinghouse website, prospective student athletes are able to access information needed to understand the Division I and II eligibility requirements, register with the Clearinghouse and access individual Clearinghouse records.

General information on the NCAA Clearinghouse website includes 1. links to the NCAA website, 2. core course listings for high schools, 3. an online version of the *NCAA Guide for the College-Bound Student-Athlete*, 4. online information about Division I and II initial eligibility requirements, and 5. online frequently-asked questions (FAQs).

Prospective student athletes also will be able to submit their Student Release Form (SRF) via the web. Registered students can update their registration information, if necessary, and also check their certification status. The toll-free number 877/262-1492 is the customer service line for the Clearinghouse; 888/388-9748 is the Publication Division; and 877/861-3003 is their 24-hour Initial Eligibility Hotline.

Seven Points to Remember about Eligibility

1. Requirements for eligibility to participate differ in Divisions I and II.

2. If you've been home-schooled during all of grades 9-12, you don't have to register with the clearinghouse. Your certification status will be determined through an initial eligibility waiver. Please contact the college or university you plan to attend for more information about the waiver process.

3. NCAA academic committees are vested with the authority to grant waivers of the initial eligibility requirements, based on objective evidence that demonstrates circumstances in which a student's overall academic record warrants the waiver of the normal application of the legislation.

4. Initial eligibility waivers must be filed by the NCAA institution on behalf of the student. (Note: Students with NCAA-approved diagnosed disabilities may file a waiver on their own behalf.)

5. Correspondence and independent study courses may be used to meet the 13 core course requirements provided the following conditions are met:

    a. the course meets all requirements for a core course as defined in the NCAA Guide);

    b. the instructor and the student have access to one another during the duration of the course for purposes of teaching, evaluating, and providing assistance to the student;

    c. evaluation of the student's work is conducted by the appropriate academic authorities in accordance with the high school's established academic policies; and

    d. the course is acceptable for any student and is placed on the high-school transcript.

6. Courses taken in the 8th grade may not be used to satisfy the core-curriculum requirements, regardless of the course or the content.

7. Students enrolling in a Division I institution generally may not use courses taken after high-school graduation to meet core curriculum requirements. (Note: Students with NCAA-approved diagnosed disabilities may use courses taken after graduation but before full-time college enrollment.)

Information above from NCAA Clearinghouse; copyright 2003 by the NCAA.

NCAA Website Lists All Colleges and Universities

The NCAA website has a complete listing of all active NCAA member colleges and universities in the U. S. They're broken down into Division 1A, Division 1AA, Division 1AAA, Division II, and Division III. Each school and its location is listed, and each is a link that you can click on to find out loads and loads of information about each and every school.

For school information, click on the lists of school and then the individual schools you want to know about after you open http:\\www.ncaa.org/sponsorships.

Photo by Marc Jablonski

Recruiting

We can't emphasize this point enough: To become a student athlete in college, you must begin preparing in the 9th grade of high school!

Before 9th grade, you become a prospective student athlete if a college gives you or your friends or relatives any financial aid or other benefits that the college does not generally give to prospective students.

You become a "recruited prospective student athlete" at a particular college if any coach or college's athletic representatives approaches you or any family member about enrolling and participating in athletics at a particular college. Activities by coaches or boosters that cause you to become a recruited prospective student-athlete are:

- an official visit by someone from the college,

- placing more than one telephone call to you or any other member of your family; or

- visiting you or someone in your family anywhere other than on the college campus.

DIVISION I RECRUITING

In addition to general recruiting regulations, no alumni, boosters, or representatives of a college's athletic interests can be involved in your recruiting. There can be no phone calls or letters from boosters. However, recruiting by alumni or representatives who are a part of the college's regular admissions program for all prospective students, including nonathletes, can contact you.

You or your family may not receive any benefit, inducement, or arrangement, such as cash, clothing, cars, improper expenses, transportation, gifts, or loans to encourage you to sign a National Letter of Intent or to attend an NCAA college.

Letters from coaches, faculty members, and students (not boosters) are not permitted until September 1 of the beginning of your junior year in high school.

TELEPHONE CALLS

In all sports other than football and basketball, phone calls from faculty members and coaches (but not boosters) are not permitted until July 1st after completion of your junior year. After this, in sports other than football, a college coach or faculty member is limited to one telephone call per week to you (or your parents or legal guardians), except that unlimited calls to you (or your parents or legal guardians) may be made under the following circumstances:

- during the five days immediately before your official visit by the college you'll be visiting,

- on the day of a coach's off-campus contact with you by that coach, and

- on the initial date for signing the National Letter of Intent in your sport through two days after the initial signing date.

Division I and I-AA football coaches may telephone you once during May of your junior year in high school and then not again until September 1. They may telephone you as often as they wish during the period 48 hours before and 48 hours after 7:00 a.m. on the initial signing date for the National Letter of Intent. Outside of a contact period, a football coach may telephone you only once a week.

Division I basketball coaches may telephone you once during March in your junior year and not again until September 1 of your senior year.

Division I ice hockey coaches may telephone a prospect who lives in a foreign country once during July after the prospect's sophomore year.

You or your parents or guardians may telephone a coach as much as you wish at your own expense. Coaches also may accept calls from you, using a toll-free number on or after July 1 after completing your junior year.

Additional information can be found in the NCAA book.

PERSONAL CONTACTS

College coaches may contact you in person off the college campus only on or after July 1 after completing your junior year. Any face-to-face meeting during which you say more than "hello" is a personal contact. Any face-to-face meeting that is prearranged or occurs at your high school, competition, or practice site is a contact, regardless of the conversation and is not permissible.

In all sports except football and basketball, coaches may contact you off the college campus no more than three times. However, a college coach may visit your high school with the approval of your principal only once a week during a contact period. Football coaches may contact you off the campus six times but not more than once a week. Ice hockey coaches have seven recruiting opportunities during the academic year but not more than three may be in-person, off-campus contacts.

OFFICIAL VISITS

Official visits (one expense-paid visit) to a particular campus comes in your senior year with no more than five such visits. It may last no longer than 48 hours and may include transportation for you and your parents, meals, lodging, complimentary admissions to campus athletic events, and perhaps a student athlete handbook.

PRINTED MATERIALS

On or after September 1 of your junior year, you may receive official academic, admissions, and student services publications; videotapes published by the college; general correspondence; game programs; media guides; and/or recruiting brochures. You could be flooded with printed materials from one college and only a few from another, depending on their recruiting programs.

OFFICIAL VISITS

You can have one official expense-paid visit to a particular campus during your senior year and no more than five in that year. This restriction applies even if you're being recruited in more than one sport. A college may not give you an official visit unless you have provided it with a PSAT, ACT, or SAT score from a test taken on a national testing date under national testing conditions.

During your official visit of no more than 48 hours, you may receive round-trip transportation between your home and the campus, and you and your parents may receive meals and lodging. You also may receive three complimentary admissions to campus athletic events. In addition, a student host may help you and your family become acquainted with campus life, and the host may spend $30 per day to cover costs of entertaining you and your parents; however, the money cannot be used to purchase college souvenirs, such as T-shirts or other mementos.

PRINTED MATERIALS

A Division II college may provide you with printed recruiting materials on or after September 1 at the beginning of your junior year. They may show you a highlight film/videotape but may not send it to you or leave it with you or your coach. A college also may provide you with a questionnaire, camp brochure, and educational information published by the NCAA at any time.

DIVISION III

Division III information can be found on page 11 of the NCAA guide. Information includes contacts, visits, and official visits.

OTHER NCAA INFORMATION

Information about amateurism issues, agents, drug testing, and graduation rates are found on page 15 of the NCAA guide. Comments about scouting services, all-star contests, transfer students, conference regulations, and reporting rule violations are found on page 12.

Questions You Should Ask

Q: What positions will I play on your team?

- It's not always obvious.
- Most coaches want to be flexible so that you're not disappointed.

Q: Describe the other players competing at the same position.

- If there's a former high-school All-American at that position, you may want to take that into consideration.
- This will give you clues as to what year you might be a starter.

Q: Can I "redshirt" my first year?

- Find out how common it is to redshirt and how that will affect graduation.
- Does the school redshirt if you're injured?

Q: What are the physical requirements each year?

- Philosophies of strength and conditioning vary by institution.
- You may be required to maintain a certain weight.

Q: How would you best describe your coaching style?

- Every coach has a particular style that involves different motivational techniques and discipline.
- You need to know if a coach's teaching style doesn't match your learning style.

Q: What is the game plan?

- For team sports, find out what kind of offense and defense is employed.

- For individual sports, find to how you are seeded and how to qualify for conference and national championships.

Q: When does the head coach's contract end?

- Don't make any assumptions about how long a coach will be at a school.

- If the coach is losing and the contract ends in two years, you may have a new coach.

Q: Describe the preferred, invited and uninvited walk-on situation. How many make it, compete, and earn a scholarship?

- Different teams treat walk-ons differently.

Q: How good is the department in my major?

- Smaller colleges can have very highly rated departments.

- A team's reputation is only one variable to consider.

Q: What percentage of players on scholarships graduate in four years?

- This will tell you about the quality of their commitment to academics.

- The team's grade point average also is a good indicator of the coach's commitment to academics.

Q: Describe the typical class size.

- At larger schools, classes are likely to be larger and taught by teaching assistants.

- Average class size is important to the amount of attention you receive.

Q: Describe in detail your academic support program. For example, study hall requirements, tutor availability, staff, class load, or faculty cooperation.

- This is imperative for marginal students.

- Find a college that will take the 3.00 students and help them get a 3.50 GPA.

Q: Describe the typical day for a student athlete.

- This will give you a good indication of how much time is spent in class, practice, studying, and traveling.

- It also will give you a good indication of what coaches expect.

Q: What are the resident halls like?

- Make sure you would feel comfortable in study areas, community bathrooms, and laundry facilities.

- Number of students in a room and coed dorms are other variables to consider.

Q: Will I be required to live on campus throughout my athletic participation?

- If the answer is yes, ask whether there are exceptions.

- Apartment living may be better than dorm living.

Q: How much financial aid is available for summer school?

- There is no guarantee. Get a firm commitment.

- You may need to lighten your normal load and go to summer school in order to graduate in four years. You can take graduate courses and maintain your eligibility.

Q: What are the details of financial aid at your institute?

- What does my scholarship cover?

- What can I receive in addition to the scholarship and how do I get more aid?

Q: How long does my scholarship last?

- Most people think a "full ride" is good for four years.

- Financial aid is available on a one-year renewable basis.

Q: If I'm injured, what happens to my financial aid?

- A grant-in-aid is not guaranteed past a one-year period even for injuries.

- It is important to know if a school has a commitment to assist student athletes for more than a year after they have been injured.

Q: What are my opportunities for employment while I'm a student?

- Find out if you can be employed in-season, out-of-season, or during vacation periods.

Scholarship Facts and Figures

Giving and receiving athletic scholarships is much more complicated than we're led to believe. Each division (I and II) has a limited number of athletic scholarships that can be given each year, so just because you think that you or your student athlete is deserving of a "full ride," it doesn't necessarily follow that it will happen. And Division III doesn't give athletic scholarships at any time.

Each school in each division must abide by NCAA rules on giving scholarships, and some athletic departments choose to give only partial scholarships, based on the number allotted for each sport. Here's how it works. Let's say you want to play football at a Division I school. Each Division I college is allowed to have only 85 football players receiving scholarships. That doesn't mean that they can give 85 every year; it means that each year, only 85 players on their team can be going to school on an athletic scholarship.

Let's say that ten seniors going to school on athletic scholarships will graduate in the spring or summer. That leaves only ten scholarships to award to incoming freshmen. Regardless of how talented you or your child may be, the chances of getting a full scholarship are based on variables (Remember that "Variable" page?).

Let's take women's basketball. Division I schools are permitted only 13 scholarships per year, and Division II schools are permitted 10, but they can be split. So only 13 Division I players can be going to school on athletic scholarships each year, but more than 10 in Division II because some players have split scholarships. However, in some sports, partial scholarships are awarded so the athletic department gets more athletes. Those students then must come up with the rest of the tuition and expenses through academic scholarships, grants, loans, or self-pay. For example, in Division II, there's a good possibility that more partial scholarships will be given to both men and women rather than full scholarships. On the next page is a breakdown of the number of athletic scholarships that can be in effect each year in both divisions according to NCAA rules in both divisions. Asterisks denote scholarships that can be split.

DIVISION I

MEN'S SPORTS

baseball—11.7*
basketball—13
CC/track—12.6*
football—85
golf—4.5*
swimming—9.9*
tennis—4.5*

WOMEN'S SPORTS

basketball—13
CC/track—16
golf—6*
gymnastics—10
soccer—11*
softball—11*
swimming—14*
tennis—8
volleyball—12

DIVISION II

MEN'S SPORTS

baseball—9*
basketball—10*
CC/track—12.6*
football—36*
golf—3.6*
soccer—9*
swimming—8.1*
tennis—4.5*
volleyball—4.5*
wrestling—9*

WOMEN'S SPORTS

basketball—10*
CC/track—12.6*
field hockey—6.3*
golf—5.4*
soccer—9.9*
softball—7.2*
swimming—8.1*
tennis—6*
volleyball—8*

* Sports that offer partial scholarships

As you can see, getting a full athletic scholarship, unless you happen to be fortunate enough to be a blue chip athlete, isn't as easy as John Q. Smith told you it is. This is why almost everyone involved with this book says that you must concentrate on *grades, grades, grades* all through high school so that you can be eligible for academic scholarships! *Information is power!*

What Are Your Chances of Hitting the Top?

Are you planning to become an All-American in college? How about going on from there to the pros? While we always urge athletes to do all it takes to reach the top, the odds are against many of them reaching athletic goals that are too often unattainable. That's why everybody hammers on education first and sports second.

As a good, average, or even Blue Chip athlete, your chances of participating in sports beyond your high-school years are slim, to say the least. We're not here to destroy your dreams, but we'd like you to be realistic about the possibilities of reaching stardom and having to duck autograph hounds all of your life.

The NCAA has compiled approximations of actual percentages of the number of athletes who reach the top. We'll give you some interesting statistics and suggest you go online at http:\\www.ncaa.org/research/prob_of_competing/ for further details.

For example, of 157,000 high-school senior student athletes playing men's basketball, only 44 will be drafted by the pros; that's *.00028 percent*. Only 2.9 percent (fewer than one in 35) will go on to NCAA college basketball, and only 1.3 percent will become professionals straight from college (fewer than one in 75).

Women basketball players have a slightly higher chance to be recruited for college: 3.1 percent of 130,500 players, but only one percent make it to the pros after college and .02 percent go straight to the pros from high school.

Football isn't a whole lot better, guys. Only 250 will be drafted out of NCAA colleges from 983,600 high school players, with 5.8 percent going to college, 2.0 percent going on to the pros from college, and .02 going straight to the pros from high school.

Baseball seems to have better odds, but there's still no guarantee. Of 455,300 high-school baseball players, 600 will be drafted out of college, with 5.6 percent playing in a NCAA member institution (one in 50), 10.5 percent (less than 11 in 100) senior males being drafted by a major league team, and only one in 200 high school seniors being drafted directly by a major league baseball team.

Men's ice hockey and men's soccer players have comparable statistics, and it appears that pinning all of your hopes on becoming a pro player isn't a good move.

Remember that these statistics are compiled with many assumptions and estimations in the process of calculation, so don't take them as exact but view them as educated calculations. But the odds are still against your making it to the pros!

National Letter of Intent

2003-04 National Letter of Intent Signing Dates
(Approved by Collegiate Commissioners Association)

Sport	Initial Date	Final Date
Basketball (Early Period)	Nov. 12, 2003	Nov. 19, 2003
Basketball (Late Period)	April 14, 2004	May 19, 2004
Football (Midyear JC tansfer)	Dec. 17, 2003	Jan. 15, 2004
Football (Regular)	Feb. 4, 2004	April 1, 2004
Field Hockey, Soccer, Men's Water Polo	Feb. 4, 2004	Aug. 4, 2004
All Other Sports (Early Period)	Nov. 12, 2003	Nov. 19, 2003
All Other Sports (Late Period)	April 14, 2004	Aug. 1, 2004

Note: These dates are subject to change

Which College Offers Which Sport?

If you're under the impression that most colleges offer a wide variety of sports, we're here to tell you that it isn't so. Does it surprise you that the top three sports across the nation are baseball, basketball, and cross country? What about football? Believe it or not, that ranks lower than golf, soccer, and tennis.

Doubt these statements? Well, the NCAA has counted them and arrived at these surprising conclusions: Basketball is the number one sport, with a total of 984 schools playing men's basketball with 1,013 women's teams under NCAA sanction. Baseball is second with 858 schools, and cross country comes in third—way ahead of football—with 853 schools. Only 617 schools have NCAA- sponsored football teams. (Information as of September 1, 2001.)

So if basketball is your sport, you have a marvelous choice of schools, provided you also like their academic programs.

If you're not into the major sports and instead concentrate on gymnastics or fencing, your choice is very narrow: Only 23 schools offer gymnastics and 36 fencing. Would you believe that 47 schools offer water polo? And only nine offer synchronized swimming. And nobody in Division I offers badminton?

This isn't meant to be funny. What we're trying to show you is that "college sports" means different things to different people, and you have to work hard to find a school that matches your special interest with a good academic program. There's that idea again—academics. I mean, how many people become pro badminton players?

Check out the NCAA website for more information at http:\\www.ncaa.org/sponsorships/sponsummary.html.

What's a "Seasonal Sport"?

Football is a fall sport; baseball is played in the spring. Yes and no. It all depends on what school you go to.

In Division I and II schools and even some Division III colleges, many sports that are played in one certain season of the year get almost year-round emphasis. For example, football players spend the summer working out as both individuals and as a team. After the season, players are expected to continue their personal workouts in the gym and weight rooms throughout the winter and spring. Baseball and track/field also require out-of-season workouts, practices, etc.

If your interest is in more than one sport, you might consider a Division III school where you can participate in two or more, since many schools don't require year-round emphasis.

The basic seasonal sports breakdown is listed below. Your job is to match your sports interest(s) with the right college.

FALL	WINTER	SPRING
cross country	basketball	baseball
football	fencing	golf
soccer	gymnastics	lacrosse
water polo (M)	ice hockey	rowing
volleyball (F)	rifle	softball
field hockey	skiing	tennis
	swimming/diving	volleyball (M)
	indoor track/field	outdoor track/field
	wrestling	water polo (F)

(M)—male
(F)—female

NCAA Student Athlete Advisory Committee Helps Shape Athletic Policies

Every division has a Student Athlete Advisory Committee (SAAC) composed of student athletes who offer insight on the student athlete experience and input on rules, regulations, and policies that shape their lives on NCAA member campuses.

The three SAACs, composed of both male and female student athletes, are responsible for providing input on issues related to student athlete welfare that are division-specific. This is the same group that compiled the questions that begin on page 246. Their guidelines include

- generating a student athlete voice within the NCAA structure,

- soliciting student athlete response to proposed NCAA legislation,

- suggesting potential NCAA legislation,

- reviewing, reacting, and commenting on the governance structure on legislation, activities, and subjects of interest,

- actively participating in the administrative process of athletics programs and the NCAA, and

- promoting a positive student athlete image.

The SAAC offers many website links to colleges and universities that have home pages. Many institutions have a section just for their athletic department. Check out www.ncaa.org/membership. A search of the web may uncover new resources for you. Try the following words to locate new websites and information: community service, student organizations, higher education, student government, student athlete welfare, or leadership.

You can also check out topics on financial aid in Divisions I and II, playing and practice limitations, Title IX, transfer rules, continuing eligibility, avenues of assistance, athletics certification, governance structure, legislative process, and athletic departments' budgets.

Some of the type of questions and answers found on this website follow:

Q: May athletics financial aid be awarded for four years? How long does an athletic scholarship last?

A: Most people think a "full ride" is good for four years. However, when a student's athletic ability is taken into consideration, financial aid may not be awarded for a period longer than one academic year.

Q: If my coach leaves, can I transfer and immediately be eligible?

A: No. Contrary to popular belief, the departure of a coaching staff member does not grant a student athlete relief from the residence requirement on transferring.

Q: What is Title IX?

A: This is an Education Amendment Act of 1972, a federal law that states: "No person in the United States shall, on the basis of sex, be excluded from participation in, be denied the benefits of, or be subjected to discrimination under any education program or activity receiving federal financial assistance."

You'll find 26 pages of questions/answers and other valuable information at this site about athletic financial aid, transfer rules, Title IX, eligibility, NCAA governance, and athletic departments' budgets (revenue and expenses). Check it out!

Recruiting Terms

ACADEMIC SPORTS STAFF—Everyone involved in helping student athletes in academic courses to maintain eligibility through good grades: administrators, tutors, and other support personnel.

ATHLETIC SCHOLARSHIP—The grant (financial aid that does not have to be paid back) that provides financial aid; grant-in-aid.

BLUE CHIP PLAYER—An athletically superior recruit who appears to be able to quickly and substantially contribute to a sports program.

BOOSTER—One who enthusiastically supports an athletic team; fan, parent, fellow student, alumnus

CAMPS AND CLINICS—One-to-five-day skill-building sessions for various sports in which student athletes gain knowledge and hands-on experience in their particular sport; usually conducted by colleges and staffed by former coaches or sports personalities.

CAMPUS VISITS—An official or unofficial visit by an athlete to a college to see the campus and meet athletic personnel. In an official visit, college provides transportation, food, and lodging and attempts to persuade the athlete to enroll in that school.

CONTACT—Any face-to-face encounter between a prospect or his/her parents/guardians and a college representative during which conversation occurs. A college coach may contact student athletes only on or after July 1 of their junior year.

CORE COURSE—An academic course offering fundamental instruction in a specific area of study (English, math, social science, natural or physical science, and additional courses, such a foreign language, computer science, philosophy, and nondoctrinal religion).

DEAD PERIOD—Length of time when recruiters can't make in-person recruiting contacts or evaluations either on or off the college's campus or encourage official or unofficial visits by prospects to the campus; telephone calls are permitted. The dead period varies for each sport, and generally surrounds the National Letter of Intent signing period, and for men's and women's basketball, the Final Four.

EARLY SIGNING PERIOD—A week in November when athletes from sports other than football can sign a National Letter of Intent.

FINANCIAL AID—Financial assistance that is not directly or overtly linked to athletic performance.

GENDER EQUALITY—Efforts made by colleges to provide athletic opportunities for women proportionate to their representation in the student population.

GRADUATION RATE—Data regarding the number and percentage of student athletes who graduated from a college or university within a six-year period.

INITIAL-ELIGIBILITY CLEARINGHOUSE—Certifies that student athletes have fulfilled their academic requirements. Registration with the clearinghouse is a requirement of NCAA Division I and II institutions only. The certification process should begin by the end of a high school student athlete's junior year.

JUCO—An abbreviation of "junior college," referring to a two-year junior or community college or players who are recruited from them.

LETTER OF INTENT—An official document that binds a student athlete to an athletic scholarship at a particular college or university.

NATIONAL LETTER OF INTENT—Administered by the Collegiate Commissioners Association, not the NCAA. Restrictions on signing a National Letter of Intent may affect a student athlete's eligibility, so be sure to read the letter carefully. It can't be signed before the National Letter of Intent signing date.

OFFICIAL VISIT—A visit during which the institution pays all or part of the student athlete's expenses, not lasting more than 48 hours; may include round-trip transportation, meals, lodging, and admission to campus athletic events for the student and parents/guardians.

PHONE CALLS—Telephone contact by a college coach, limited to one per week to the student athlete and his/her family.

PROPOSITION 48—The requirement that says a student athlete must attain minimum test scores in ACT and SAT, as well as qualifying grades in specific core academic courses.

PROSPECT—A student athlete beginning in the 9th grade. Before 9th grade, student athletes become prospects if a college gives them or their relatives any financial aid or other benefits that a college doesn't generally provide to prospective students.

QUALIFIER—A prospective student athlete who's already met grade requirements in core academic courses, along with minimum qualifying scores on either SAT or ACT.

QUESTIONNAIRE—A document that asks an athletic prospect a variety of personal, academic, and athletic information.

RECRUITED PROSPECTIVE STUDENT ATHLETE—A student athlete who has been approached by a coach or representative of a college's athletic interests to enroll and participate in athletics at that college.

RECRUITING—The college process of identifying, contacting, evaluating, persuading, and signing potential student athletes.

RECRUITING CALENDAR—The annual sequence of periods during which coaches may contact prospects by mail or phone, when prospects' schools and homes may be visited, and when recruits may sign National Letters of Intent.

RECRUITING GURU—A writer, public broadcaster, or analyst who closely follows the recruiting process and offers information and opinions on an athlete's abilities, the prospect's chosen schools, and the success recruits have had in fulfilling their recruiting needs.

RECRUITING NUT—Someone involved with a certain school as a fan or alumnus so fascinated with its athletic fortunes that he/she seizes upon every bit of information about the school's new recruits.

STUDENT RELEASE FORM—The NCAA Initial Eligibility Clearinghouse's form that authorizes the student athlete's high school to send a transcript, test scores, and other academic information to the clearinghouse and authorizes it to send the information to colleges that the student athlete has listed on the form if the college requests it.

TEST SCORES—The scores received by players on their standardized ACT or SAT tests. A student must get a minimum of 700 on the SAT or 17 on the ACT, along with at least a 2.50 GPA to be eligible for any sports participation.

TRANSFER STUDENT—A student athlete who transfers from one school to another while still intending to compete in a particular sport.

UNOFFICIAL VISIT—A time when a student athlete visits a particular school at his/her own expense an unlimited number of times before his/her senior year.

VERBAL COMMITMENT—An announced intent by an athlete to accept a scholarship form, sign a Letter of Intent, to enroll and compete at a particular school. Verbal commitments are not binding on recruits.

WALK-ON—A player who enrolls at a school and participates in a particular sport without first receiving an offer of a scholarship or other financial aid.

WRITTEN CORRESPONDENCE—College coaches may not write to a student athlete before September 1 of his/her junior year. However, NCAA educational information, camp brochures, and questionnaires may be sent before this time.

SUMMARY

Summary

This book is exactly what it's called—*a guide*. It's intended to give you information, but *you* have to do the work if you want a scholarship or financial aid. The info we've presented will benefit any athlete in any sport, male or female. The more information you can gather, the better your understanding and chances of getting a scholarship and/or financial aid.

The recruiting process is basically the same for all high-school student athletes, with the differences being in the colleges themselves and their particular division level or type of program. Understand which college sports generate money and offer full scholarships and which ones offer only partial scholarships or financial aid.

The common denominators are emphasized by all of the individuals who were gracious enough to *give something back to the game* by taking the time to offer you advice:

1. focus on grades, grades, grades;

2. get yourself noticed, be prepared for every opportunity, play hard the entire game, and be a well-rounded person;

3. follow your dreams but be realistic about your abilities, make sure you have a "Plan B" to fall back on, and *get a college education*.

You can't go wrong if you take the advice of ESPN's football analyst Paul Maguire to start out by making your "Plan A" the goal of getting a college education and your "Plan B" your dream of playing sports at the next level, whether it's collegiately or professionally.

Set your goals with definite plans on how to implement them; understand the "variables" factor; do whatever it takes to get yourself noticed; learn what questions to ask; be sure you earn the best possible grades, starting in junior high; know the eligibility rules; understand how to conduct and promote yourself when you communicate with college coaches; and *continuously strive to improve yourself daily both athletically and academically!*

Keep in mind that every recruiting situation is different. The athletic recruiting process is not an exact science; there is NO step-by-step process to follow that guarantees you a sports scholarship. Unless you are in the same category of Lebron James talentwise, it's up to YOU to separate yourself from the pack.

An excellent example of a naturally good athlete making himself a great athlete is Maurice Clarett, a running back from Ohio's Warren Harding High School, who was chosen as the 2001 *USA TODAY*'s Offensive High-school Player of the Year."

Maurice Clarett, with the help of his mother, set goals at an early age and mapped out a plan on how to reach his particular dream. When Maurice's Mother, Michelle, who raised him in a single-parent household, was asked: "When did Maurice begin pursuing his dreams and taking sports seriously?", she answered: "In first grade, Maurice's teacher asked everybody in his class to stand up and tell their classmates what they wanted to be when they grew up. Maurice said he wanted to be a professional football player."

As Maurice grew older, his knowledge and love for the game also grew. He understood that he needed to set goals and work hard to achieve his dreams. In junior-high school in Youngstown, Ohio, he realized the true meaning of an athlete playing sports for the love of the game. He knew that he had to have a love for the game at all times, not just while playing a game but also during practices, watching game films, lifting weights and running in the off-season, while in the classroom or studying at home, and most important, when the self-discipline is necessary to avoid the temptations that can appear during a high-school student's social life.

To take the steps necessary for Maurice to reach his goals, he mapped out a daily workout and study plan that he would follow religiously. Mike Butch, Jr., Maurice's 7th- and 8th-grade basketball and football coach says, "Maurice Clarett would not allow his work ethic and discipline to be second to anyone's. He was always concerned that there may be somebody else out there who may be trying harder than he was." Coach Butch says that what made Maurice special and separated him from other good athletes is that he would always stay after practice to work on his game. In basketball, he would stay to work on his conditioning by running wind sprints. His day still wasn't over when he left the field or the gym; after his mother would pick him up from practice, Maurice would have her drive him to the local YMCA so that he could work out in the fitness center and play basketball in the gym. *Are you willing to make that same commitment to excellence?*

When it comes to receiving an athletic scholarship, the bottom line comes down to numbers and talent. "There are only so many scholarships available, and it comes down to either you being good enough or not."

If the time comes where you don't receive an athletic scholarship and you feel that you were overlooked, then it's up to you to walk on at a college, make the team, and earn a scholarship just as many other great athletes, such as Jason Giambi of the New York Yankees and Jeremy Shockey of the New York Giants had to do.

If you have to go the route of walking on at a college to try to earn a scholarship in your freshman, sophomore, junior, or senior year, then a good grade-point average in high school is going to come in extremely handy when it comes time to apply for the financial aid needed for you or to pay for your college tuition so that you can continue pursuing your athletic dreams.

Another great example of a good high-school athlete who was overlooked in the recruiting process is Zack Walz. Zack, a former Arizona Cardinals' linebacker who is interviewed in this book, had the initiative as a high-school student athlete to take it upon himself to promote his athletic and academic abilities to colleges all across the United States. His opportunity to play college football came at Dartmouth College, which is a member of the Ivy League. The Ivy League conference does not allow its members to offer athletic scholarships. The moral of this story is that Zack's hard work in the classroom during high school paved the way for him to be able to receive financial assistance to accept Dartmouth's offer and go on to have a tremendous collegiate and professional career.

The best advice I can give today's student athletes is that they need to attend sports camps. The instructors at these camps will not only help them improve their game, but they will also help them understand the importance of having a college education to fall back on when their playing days are over.

Photo by John Young

One of my favorite quotes about self-improvement that I have shared with players that I've coached along the way comes from Steve Young, the former quarterback for the San Francisco 49ers who graduated from Brigham Young University. Basically what Steve said was,

"Student Athletes need to compete against themselves;
it's about self-improvement;
it's about being better today than they were the day before."

Photo by Diane Wilding

Special Thanks

I'd like to take this time to thank all of the special individuals who made this guide possible. Three special people believed in my idea of writing this athletic and academic scholarship guide to benefit student athletes of the future and their parents.

First, I'd like to thank my mom, Georgiana, for all of her help, patience, and support throughout the period of time it took me to write this guide and for her understanding of why I wrote it in memory of my dad, Michael, to whom I dedicate this book.

Second, the lady behind the scenes, actually behind the words, was Diane Wilding, the editor, who made the entire guide possible by believing in my idea from the beginning and the concept of why it was being written. Diane went far beyond the call of duty with her involvement in this guide because she sincerely believed that she was a part of something special—a guide that can help thousands of youngsters and their parents across the country to understand the realities of athletic scholarships and the importance of getting a good college education while saving some money in the process.

Third, I'd like to thank Bobby Jones for believing in me and my idea. Bobby was the first person I interviewed about his thoughts on the athletic recruiting process, professional sports, and the importance of getting a college education. Bobby's interview was not only the most inspirational, considering that he never gave up on his dreams of making it to the NFL, but it was also the most significant. It always seems to take one person on a team to be a believer and a leader for the rest of the team to follow. Once Bobby's interview was printed and shown to the other interviewees, everything else fell into place, and it snowballed after that.

Thanks to all of the people who took the time to express their feelings verbally or on paper about their experiences in order to benefit young athletes and their parents. Hundreds of high school, collegiate, and professional athletes, coaches, and scouts, as well as parents offered valuable input.

Special thanks to Jimmy Valentini, who designed the book cover; Bob Thompson, a parent experiencing the recruiting process firsthand, acted as consultant; and Tracey Bodnar, owner of WildInkMouse Productions, who designed the website; Dave and Mary Jane Pettola, Jennifer Kaizer, Ashley Orr and Brandi Panning from Progressive Printing; Ken Abel, ABELexpress Publishing; Budd Bailey; Allison Gatta; Bill Oliver; Jim Szuch; Dodie Ownes; Tom & Marilyn Ross; Avery Cardoza from Cardoza Publishing; and Hilda Maaskant from R.R. Bowker, who offered valuable advice during the publishing process; and to Jerry Bonkowski and John Delcos for writing the forewords.

Special thanks also goes out to all the individuals, businesses and high schools who were gracious enough to provide pictures for this book; Cindy Zordich, John Young, Marc "Joe Kodak" Jablonski, Bob Knuff, Memory Lane Photography, Jeff Bayuk of Hubbard High School, Paul Gregory of Cardinal Mooney High School, Wayne Bair of Brookfield High School, Dino Balkan, Adeline Timko, Shirley Libeg, Robert Thompson, Rich Delisio, Mike Butch Jr., John Caparanis of ESPN Sports radio 1240 AM, Mike Case of NBC's WFMJ TV, and Dave Burcham, sports editor for the *Tribune Chronicle* in Warren, Ohio.

And last, but not least, Andrew Kreutzer, Ph. D., coordinator of the Ohio University Sports Administration Program. This program is known to be one of the best, if not *the* best, sports administration program in the U. S. A. for 35 years. Andy certainly proved to me how special this program was by networking me with valuable contacts to every possible avenue involved with high-school, collegiate, and professional sports programs. He supplied me with needed connections to the NCAA to ensure that information in this guide was in compliance with NCAA rules and regulations.

All I needed were Andy's program alumni directory and his name as a reference, and every alum I contacted was eager to give me information for this guide. After my dealings with Dr. Kreutzer and his program, which includes Greg Gulas, Class of '78, I can't imagine a better program in the country. Once again, I'm proud to be an Ohio University Bobcat alumnus.

—*Mark Bercik*

Index

academic eligibility requirements *233-238*
academic scholarship *145, 175*
academic sports staff *259*
academic support program *46-47, 99-100, 248*
athletic directors *121-122, 149-151*
athletic scholarship *100-101, 258-259*
attitude *79-82, 86, 90-92, 97, 149-151, 160*
Blue Chip player *9, 124, 252-253, 259*
book information *18, 78, 81, 148, 223*

camps *48, 60, 62, 83-84, 91, 117, 149, 151*
campus life information *230*
campus visits *44-46, 79, 244-246, 259-261*
college All-Americans *41, 61-62, 68-68, 78-81, 85, 86-88, 90, 93*
                              124-127, 157-160, 161-162, 165-166

college coaches *63-67, 82-84, 93-96, 100-102, 113-115*
                              170-175, 217-219
college information *229*
college scouting services *180*
communication skills *118, 150, 187-188*
contact (recruiting) *244, 259*
core course/GPA *97, 148, 233-240, 259*

dress code *118, 150*

early signing period *260*
educational information *229*
evaluation (recruiting) *171*

financial aid information *227-228, 249, 260*

gender equality *260*
graduation rate *96, 102, 247, 260*
guidance counselor *144-148, 232*

high-school All-Americans *97, 130-134, 265*
high-school coaches *82-84, 93-96, 97-112, 113-115, 116-120*
                              121-122, 135-136, 144-148, 149-151, 152-153

internet videos/recruiting and scouting services *174, 181-182*
introductory letter *187-188*

junior college (Juco) *52-53, 82-84, 115, 173, 260*

junior high school information 48, 79, 83, 95, 114, 118, 124
135-136, 138, 141, 160

men's sports 252, 255-256

National Letter of Intent 103, 254, 260
NCAA advice and information 148, 234-262
NCAA Clearinghouse 147-148, 239-260
NCAA eligibility requirements 147-148, 233-239
NCAA membership sports 254-259

parents/guardians (interviews) 118, 135, 139, 141, 156-168
174, 224-227
parents' role 47, 56, 76, 79-80, 83, 87-88, 121, 135, 145
147, 166, 212-215, 224-227
printed materials (recruiting) 244-246
professional baseball 39, 61-62, 63-67, 82-84, 113-115
127-128, 135-136, 163-164, 165
professional coaches 63-67, 113-115
professional contracts 30, 65, 90-91, 113-115
128-129, 163-164, 165-166
professional football 54-60, 68-69, 71-73, 74-77, 78-81, 85
86-88, 89, 106-111, 124-126 157-160, 165-166
professional scouts 61-62, 67, 90-91, 113-115, 142, 167-168

qualifier 261
questionnaire 189-191, 261

recruiting terms 261
recruiting publications 180
recruiting services 84, 100, 172, 176-182
redshirt 247

scholarship advisors 153-154, 223, 228-230
sports information director 217-219
sportswriter 217-219
Student Athlete Advisory Committee 257-258
student release form 147-148, 262
telephone calls (recruiting) 243, 261
transfer student 53, 82-84, 130, 165-166, 173, 258, 262
TV analysts 71-73, 74-77

videotaping 59, 69, 173, 182, 185-186, 192-205, 215
walk-on 53, 57, 63, 130, 137-140, 263, 266
website information 146-148, 220-224, 232, 239, 241, 255-257
women's sports 120-122, 147, 254-255, 255-256

How to Contact Us

America's Complete Sports Scholarship Guide

www.AthleticScholarshipBook.com

If you have any questions or remarks, feel free to contact us at

Info@AthleticScholarshipBook.com
(330) 448-0866 • Fax: (330) 448-0936

or write to

AMERICA SPORTS PUBLISHING
6881 Stewart Road / P. O. Box 132,
Brookfield, OH 44403

Michael Zordich, Philadelphia Eagles
Photo by Cindy Zordich

We wish you the best of luck in your journey through the athletic recruiting adventure.

Follow your dreams! And hit the books!